Caste and Gender Equality in Contemporary India

Caste and Gender Equality in Contemporary India

Ed.

Dr. Anji A

Dr. A. Ranjithkumar

KALPAZ

ISBN : 978-93-5324-271-8

First Published, 2020

Published by

Kalpaz Publications
C-30, Satyawati Nagar,
Delhi – 110052
Ph.: 011-47034999, 9811692060
www.kalpazpublications.com
E-mail: kalpaz@hotmail.com

Printed at: G. Print Process, Delhi

Contents

Preface

This Edited volume is discussing about a very burning issues of our Indian society. The caste and gender discrimination is one of the main causes for social inequality in our country. It has an origins in the early Vedic times; then it was an existence in the form of Varna system which was divided the society in four divisions. Some useless people were done and did not realised about Caste system was not originally determined by birth but became in a course of time. Thus, one could be born only as a Brahmin or Kshatriya, not become one by one's deeds. Because of its rules, the caste system resulted a lot of evils. The society was divided into strict compartments and those were belonging to the higher castes hands, and they exploited the lower caste people. Still they very strongly followed untouchables in form of all the menial tasks. Politicians are encouraging and exploiting their attitudes for their own gains. Discrimination has against a low-castes peoples widely prevalent and it has kept a large percentage of our population backward. It perhaps one of the main causes for India's backwardness. Many social reformers such as Dr. B.R. Ambadkar, E.V.R. Periyar, Raja Rammohan Roy, Swami Dayanand Saraswati etc., has been tried to end caste as well as gender discrimination. So many leaders of our independent India were also against this systems. Our constitution also made a many illegal formation in caste and gender discrimination. We are thinking about the revolutions, movements, developments of science and technology and also progress in industry had changed the outlook of the people to get great extent from this discriminations and violations. But it's not true, still very highly prevalent even educated also. The caste and gender system has been weakened, but it still has considerable power, particularly among the rural people. Thus, it has not been totally rooted out. Those subjected the heaviest burden of discrimination are from the Dalit or "Scheduled Castes", known in less liberal democratic times as the "Untouchables". The name may be banned but pervasive negative attitudes of mind remain, as do the extreme levels of abuse and servitude experienced by Dalit. They experience multiple levels of discrimination and exploitation are expressing the attitude of barbaric, degrading, appallingly violent and totally inhumane.

Gender inequality has been a social issue in India and also it has continue in every field, like sociologically, economically, politically, education and health. Protection or participation of the girl child is always treated unequally. Indian society still hasn't been awakened to the importance of empowering of the women. The lot of statistics still narrate a grim story of female foeticide, girl child discrimination and gender bias. According to the Global Gender Gap Report released by the World Economic Forum (WEF) in 2011, India was ranked 113 on the Gender Gap Index (GGI) among 135 countries polled. Since then, India has improved its rankings on the World Economic Forum's Gender Gap Index (GGI) to 105/136 in 2013. The Constitution of India has several provisions and privileged which is grant certain fundamental rights to its citizen, which includes right to equality. So lot of questions were arising in the sea of thought. What gender discrimination in India means for the society? What young generation thinks about gender discrimination? Does it really exist in the modern society? Where government and society are doing lots of work to fade this gap between male and female? So, just to lighten our heart, we decided to display to our society. Some of the answers were really interesting and some of them still believing in the old thought of gender inequalities. A young mind told that the correct definition of gender discrimination is based on gender or sex in various forms like sexual harassment, unequal pay for women doing the same job as men, pregnancy determination and unequal opportunity for the male and female child in the family etc can be summed as discrimination or inequality between genders. The first and foremost cause that leads to discrimination in India is the mental makeup. Some people are thing "Women are the best fit for homes", this statement is enough to show that even with so much of technological and educational advancement, the mental status of people in India hasn't changed much. This could be attributed to the social stigma attached to women that their responsibility is only to give birth and take care of the family. The second cause may be that patriarchal society, so its clearly pointed out that 'lack of education' is the root cause of all evils and it is true also. Most of the women are in India unaware of their rights because of they are still in illiterate. For a woman to properly exercise her right, their first needs to know about it. Education is the first step of that direction. Many women would have question that; is the education enough tool to fight with the evil of gender discrimination? which one is so deep rooted in India, but the answer is NO. Education is a start but if we really want to put an end to this evil then we need to change ourselves, our mindset and harmful beliefs that we have been living with. Advocating for education and equal opportunities for women is not enough. In fact, we need to be the channels and mediums for new reforms and campaigns for empowering the women in India. Hence, our ***SATHIYAM SOCIAL SERVICE ORGANISATION*** **(SSSO) was jointly conducted with Islamiah college.** One Day National Seminar On "*Gender and Caste in Contemporary India: Issues & Challenges*" **held on 29th March 2019.** The next steps of SSSO has taken a initiative part was selected papers and bring to the publication which was received for seminar in the reputed publication of Kalpaz. Hence, we thank to all paper presenter, Board of SSSO members and those who were directly and indirectly helped for a successful of this programme and publication.

List of Contributors

1. M. Amrith Full time Research scholar & Dr. L. Rathakrishnan Professor, Department of Rural Industries and Management, Gandhigram Rural Institute.
2. Aggi Mary Anto, M. Phil. (Full-Time), Research Scholar, Department of History, St. Joseph's College (Autonomous), Tiruchirappalli
3. Kabilan. I.V, VITSOL, VIT Chennai
4. Ajesh George, M Phil (Full Time) Scholar, Department of History, St. Joseph's (Autonomous) College, Tiruchirappalli
5. Ancymol joy, M. Phil. (Full-Time), Research Scholar, Department of English, St. Joseph's College (Autonomous), Tiruchirappalli.
6. Dr. M H Hullur, Teaching Assistant, Research Centre for Women's Studies, Karnatak Universaity, Dharwad.
7. Dr. T.S. Bala Gomala, PDF WM , UGC-New Delhi & Dr. S. Baluchamy, professor & Head, Gandhigram Rural Institute
8. Joel Oommen Muzhangody, Research Scholar, Government College Kodencheri, Kozhikode, University of Calicut
9. Dr. Prabudha S. Kamble Teaching Assistant, Department of Anthropology Karnatak University Dharwad.
10. Prof. Dr. Shubhada Mohan Kulkarni KCES's Institute of Management and Research, Jalgaon, Maharashtra,
11. V. Vijaya Lakshmi, Research Assistant. DSNLU.
12. Dr. Anji A, Teaching Assistant, Research Centre for Women's Studies, Karnatak Universaity, Dharwad &

Dr. J. Balamurugan, PDF Scholar, Department of Rural Industries and Management, The Gandhigram Rural Institute

13. V. Manjuvani Research Scholar, Dept. of Law, SPMVV, Tirupathi
14. Dr. A. Ranjithkumar Research Associate, National Law School of India University (NLSIU), Bangalore & Dr. K. BARATHIRAJA,Guest Faculty, Department of Politics and International Studies, Pondicherry University, Puducherry
15. M. Eswari, Researach Associate & Research Scholar, Centre for Women's Studies, Gandhigram Rural Institute
16. Nagappa L H, Guest Faculty, Research Centre for Women's Studies, Karnatak Universaity, Dharwad.
17. Mr. Vishwanath M Ainapur, Asst. Teacher Govt. Kannada Boy's School Raibag
18. Dr. K. Pushpam, PDF (ICSSR) & Dr. R. Subburama N, Professor, Centre for lifelong learning and extension, Gandhigram Rural Institute- Deemed to be University, Gandhigram
19. Anagha Nair 3rd Year B.A LLB (Hon's), Niranjana J Anil 2 ND year, B.A, LL. B(Hons.) and Binitha M Abi, VIT School of Law University, Chennai Campus
20. Parvoti Boli, Research Scholar, Department of Geography, Rajiv Gandhi University, Itanagar, Arunachal Pradesh
21. Sheela Mathi Vathani G. M. Phil Research Scholar, Development Sociology, Gandhigram Rural Institute
22. Dr. Sukumaran. M, Assistant Professor of Economics, Dr. R. Ambedkar Memorial Govt. Arts & Science College Balussery, Koxhikode Keerala. & Dr.Santhosh Areekkuzhiyil, Assistant Professor in Educational Psychology, Government College of Teacher Education Kozhikode, Kerala.
23. Rairaj H Nagaral, Research Scholar, Dept of Sociology, Karnatak University.

Introduction

Dr. A. Anji,
Dr. A. Ranjithkumar

The aim of this edited book is to provide a comprehensive picture of the link between caste and gender in our society. Understanding the subordination of women and also the superiority enjoyed by men within the socio-cultural and economic realms is extremely vital because it expressly brings out how caste stratification and gender stratification interact one another. The suppression of girls in the past was considered essential for maintenance of caste hierarchy. Men is all communities derive pleasure from a substantial dominance over women in all spheres of life. Subordination of girls is significant feature at most stages of recorded history and is widely practiced on a mass scale over the globe. This subordination is culturally created and maintained at material and ideological levels, reinforcing the opposite (Nakkeeran 2003). What's a more important to recollect here is that although subordination of girls could be a universal development, the extent and nature of subordination of girls is conditioned by their social, economic and cultural surroundings Gender is, thus, not a monolithic class.

It is time to debate on gender and caste Gender Equality means men and women have equal opportunities for realizing their full human rights and for contributing to, and cashing in on, economic, social, cultural and political development. Gender equality is thus treating men only women equally by the society as they play similar roles, therefore the roles play in society should support ladies and men being full partners in their home, their community and their society. Gender Equality is the process of being honest to men and girls to confirm fairness. Measures should typically be taken to make amends for the historical and social disadvantages that forestall ladies and men from operating on their taking part in the field. Equity may be a means for equality and equity the result. The planet has achieved progress towards gender equality and ladies's authorisation underneath the Millennium Development Goals three and Sustainable Development Goal fifth. Even though, women are still suffering discrimination and violence in each a part of the world (MDG report 2017). Gender equality isn't solely a basic right. However it is a necessary foundation for a peaceful, prosperous world. Sadly, at the present time, one in five ladies and women between the ages of 15-49 has remained experiencing physical or sexual violence by an intimate partner. Forty nine countries presently haven't any laws protecting women from violence. Progress is going on concerning harmful practices like kid wedding and FGM (Female venereal Mutilation), has declined by 30% within the past decade. However, there's still a lot of work to be done to fully eliminate such practices. Providing ladies and women with equal access to education, healthcare, right to work, and participation in political and economic decision-making The processes can fuel property economies and profit societies and humanity at massive scale. Implementing new legal frameworks concerning feminine equality within the geographical point and therefore the destruction of harmful practices targeted at ladies is crucial to ending the gender-based discrimination prevailing in several countries round the world (UN report 2017). According to the Constitution of India: There is the right of a girl to gender equality underneath Article fourteen. Therefore the difference is the woman's right to life and dignity under Article twenty one. Except for this provision and privileges as given by the Indian constitution for protecting and empowering women. Authorisation is concerning folks each ladies and men taking management over their lives: setting their own agendas, gaining skills, building assurance, resolution issues and developing autonomy. Nobody will empower another: Solely the individual can empower herself or himself to create selections or to talk out. However, establishments as well as international cooperation agencies can support processes which will nurture self-empowerment of people or teams.

Similarly, class structure is also a development associated with Hinduism specially. Its origin, evolution and existence are peculiar to Asian nation. Class structure may be a system very much like western conception of racism wherever folks are discriminated against. Thanks to their skin colour; equally, in class structure, discrimination is completed on the idea of birth i.e. a person's social rank is outlined on the idea of his/her caste within which he/she took birth which is that the sole criterion of creating his/her social status. In different words, on the idea of caste, it's mounted at the time of a person's birth that whether or not she/he would have higher or low status in social hierarchy. Caste is the most confused knot of all social issues. Faith is simply a belief amendment anytime of the life, however caste may be a constant that don't involve amendment. Even occupation and social rank changes. Class structure is crammed with difference and injustice. There's no purpose in casteism as a system or a method. Rather it's an evil. Indian society is forged ridden. The folks of one caste don't wish to combine with others. The Manusmitri is without doubt the foremost authoritative one, legitimizing social exclusion and introducing absolute difference because the tenet of social relations.

The class structure may be a nice social evil. The class structure can not be eradicated while not ever-changing the outlook of the folks. From time to time social reformers and thinkers have tried to eradicate this evil, however to no avail. Even, Gandhiji couldn't do a lot of for the destruction of Untouchability. It's a planted drawback that has defied all solutions thus far. The matter has persisted for the most part owing to the illiteracy and cognitive content of the folks. Their cognitive content makes the folks conservative and irrational. Thence they are doing not a little for any social amendment. They need things to continue as they reach live of people. Social reform is powerfully opposed and is taken into account to be an attack on their faith by the spiritual fanatics.

It's a giant shame that even in this very twenty first century and during this age and time. Human society has so progressed scientifically that folks are attending to purchase lands on planet Mars, Indian society believes in a very system as archaic because of the class structure. There are varied social movements and notable social reformers United Nations agency have throughout their lives worked to get rid of this discriminatory system exclusively. However, not a lot of is going on the bottom. Indian Constitution conjointly provides many provisions to secure rights of socially backward persons and there are laws too in this regard however there's little be done. Still condition on the idea of caste is that the main reason behind varied styles of exploitation against supposed lower castes, particularly those delineate as Sudras and Untouchables. From the start of this technique. Sudras and untouchables were treated as slaves by supposed higher castes. They were allowed solely to try and do menial works. They got no powers or privileges. All the privileges were for Brahmanas and Kshatriyas. All the leadership position in faith, polity, economy or society was assumed and brought hold off by two of the supposed higher castes; their political or social influence was continuously tokenism. But there have been varied social reformers like Raja Ram Mohan Roy. United Nations agency devoted their lives for the upliftment of those downtrodden folks. Varied reform movements were there to get rid of the class structure. However it had been thus constituted in our social material that it was next to possible to alter truth on ground. Thus, once Asian nation got independence and therefore the Constitution was being framed, our original fathers were of the opinion that such provisions ought to be within the text which might reduce the ills of class structure and convey concerning equality in social field. Social justice was one amongst the objectives of our Constitution. Initial by the Preamble to the Constitution envisions Asian nation as a nation wherever socio-economic and political justice is there; where there'll be equality of standing and chance and where dignity of the individual is secured. The Constitution guarantees equality before law (Art. 14), and enjoins upon the State to not discriminate against any national on grounds of caste (Art. 15 (1). Untouchability is abolished and its observance in any form is impermissible (Art. 17). The Constitution mandates that no national shall, on grounds solely of caste or race, be subjected to any incapacity and restriction (Art. 15 (2). It empowers the State to create provisions for reservation in academic establishments (Art. fifteen (4) and (5)), and in appointments for posts in favour of SCs (Art. 16 (4), 16(4A), 16(4B) and Art. 335). Reservation of seats for SCs within the Lok Sabha is provided underneath Article 330, within the State Assemblies underneath Article 332 and in the native Self-Governments bodies under Articles 243D and 340T. Further, the Constitution guarantees protection from social injustice and every one varieties of exploitation (Art. 46).

Class structure in Asian nation is thus bolt planted in its socio-cultural and spiritual life that it currently virtually has God-given approval behind it. And something against or contrary to this technique is taken into account to be a sin or disrespectful to God. However actually it's no God-send virtue to be followed by the folks. It had many exploitive and discriminatory effects on our social order throughout the ages. As a by-product, class structure has given many different social ills to the society like Untouchability. The system remains continued in Asian nation as a well-established and sacred customary rule and is followed by virtually everybody despite their economic or social rank. Though the younger generation is discarding such social norms however still the system is well-entrenched in our socio-religious beliefs. Asian nation cannot become a very trendy country within the twenty first century; if it fails to get rid of this discriminatory observation supported by caste. Therefore, the sole remedy to class structure or the only means to destroy casteism is that the destruction of the faith of the Shrutis. Many international human rights organizations insist that worldwide over 260/million folks suffer from discrimination supported by caste (or 'work and descent', the international organization nomenclature for such systems of genetic status), that caste is "a basic determinant of social exclusion and development", and affects some 20–25 % of the world's population – as well as (but not restricted to) the peoples of South Asian nations and their diasporas. The predominant importance of informal processes is why social action (confined to the formal sector) isn't the central story here, albeit (as noted) the difficulty of public sector "reservations" has return to dominate national discourse and political action on caste, being attention for anxieties concerning survival or success within the post-reform economic order. It's painful that one's caste continues to stick to one's identity throughout one's life. It's a live social expertise in Asian nation than a well thought over mode of social classification and Indian society has placed caste convention intact and alive. Therefore, what Sharankumar Limbale says is extremely a true, "A feeling of rebellion is invariably among an extreme psychological commitment. As Dalit sensibility seeks to evoke compatible changes within the social consciousness, it's rebellious likewise as essentially optimistic and revolutionary". (Limbale, 1992: 267). The Sustainable Development Goals (SDGs) emphasize equality of chance and reducing difference of outcomes, the elimination of discrimination in law, policy and social observe, and socio-economic inclusion of all underneath the banner goal 'to leave no one behind'.

Therefore, if the evil of class structure is to be eradicated effort ought to be mode to teach the folks and therefore produce a powerful belief against the evil. Lessons ought to be enclosed to show the scholars that the class structure is manmade. The largest drawback in abolishing and removing this menace from the society is that the generally social acceptableness of identical. Till and unless this changes no hope is there. As a result of law will offer protection from exploitation; however it cannot bring attitudinal amendment in supposed higher castes. The young and trendy generation is probably the sole hope in transformation concerning the $64000 which means of social justice in our country.

This book is closely looking at two aspect of gender and caste issues and challenges in India. A total of twenty two papers has been collected and discussed in this volume. There are twenty articles discussing in this book from different perspectives on gender and caste. Following research papers are being discussed in this book 'the Indian Family Business And Its Contributions To Nations Development' (Amrith and Rathakrishnan), 'A Study On Constraints In Tribal Education: With Special Reference To Paniyasin Kerala' (Aggi Mary Anto), 'Functions Of Local Self Government In Infrastructure Development With Respect To Women' (Kabilan.I.V), 'Re-Ordering The Ordained: The Role Of Organized Priestly Training Of The Syrian Catholic Community In The Social Formation And The Upliftment Of The Weaker Sections Of Kerala' (Ajesh George), 'Eco-feminism: The Reflection Of The Affinity Between The Subjugation Of Women And The Human Domination Of Nature In The Society' (Ancymol Joy), 'Skill Development In Indian Through Feminist Perspectives' (M.H. Hullur), 'A Study on Elected Representatives of Dalit Women and Human Rights Prespective' (T.S. Bala Gomala and S. Baluchamy), 'Working Women: Issues And Challenges' (V. Vijaya Lakshmi), 'Women Empowerment:

Opportunities and Challenges' (Prabudha S. Kamble), 'Women Participation In Rotary Clubs' (Shubhada Mohan Kulkarni), 'Issues And Challenges Faced By Working Women' (V. Vijaya Lakshmi), 'Women And Livelihood Security Through Migration: Experiences From South India' (Anji. A), 'Impact of Climate Change on Women, Gender Equality In Contemporary India: Issues And Challenges' (V. Manjuvani), 'The Role of Gram Sabha to Promote the Social Justice: A Case of Tamil Nadu' (A. Ranjithkumar and K. Barathiraja), 'Causes of Girl Children Drop-Out In Rural Areas – An Analysis' (M. Eswari), 'An Analysis of Women Empowerment In Various Fields In India' (Nagappa L H), 'Role of Education In Empowerment of Rural Women' (K. Pushpam and R. Subburaman), 'Legalizing Prostitution: The Flip Side of A Coin' (Anagha Nair, Niranjana J Anil, Binitha M Abi), 'Socio-Economic Status of Female Manual Labor Employees At Government Institute' (Parvoti Boli), 'Barriers Faced By Elderly Women Destitudes–An Insight Into The Psycho-Social Issues A Case Study on St. Joseph Hospice, Dindigul District' (Shella Mathu Vatheni), and 'Overviews On Women Migration And Gender Issues, (Vishwanath M Ainapur). Visions of Dr. B.R. Ambedkar in the Emancipation of Tribes in India: Discourse on the Inefficient Interference of Institutions (Dr. Sukumaran. M* & Dr. Santhosh Areekkuzhiyil) and Social Development through Welfare Policies in Karnataka: Special Reference to Marriages Schemes (Mr. Raviraj H Nagaral)

The book concludes that Caste is one amongst the basic establishments of Hindu society. The importance of gender in understanding the class structure and therefore the approach caste invades on women's life cannot be unheeded. Indian society is powerfully patriarchy. Women's compliance to structure of caste and sophistication isn't simply passive. However it will reach incitement of their men folk to carry on to undisputed social power that they need wielded into modern times. Women in India are treated as inferior and lowly by their male counterparts. Women are treated as subordinates and their sex is controlled by men. In India class structure is a very important establishment. This feature makes the Indian society extremely stratified and hierarchal. Caste and gender are extremely related. Though girls of higher caste face gender discrimination at each step of their life. Nonetheless women of higher caste are entitled to bound privileges. It's vital to notice that these privileges are granted to them only they adjust to the patriarchy order of society. Women of the lower caste are the foremost deprived heap. They're victim of each gender discrimination and caste difference.

1

The Indian Family Business and Its Contributions to Nations Development

— *M. Amrith*
Dr. L. Rathakrishnan

Abstract

In the contemporary business environment, family business is the key for the welfare and development of the nation. It is imperative for the integrated economic improvement in all spheres of the country. It is understood from the family-owned companies are located in India which is 108 companies. However, in China it is 167, USA holds 121, and in France recorded upto 70 companies. In India it is accounted 25 per cent of Corporation Sales, 32 per cent of Profits after Tax (PAT), 18 per cent of assets and over 37 per cent of reserves. At present 50 families are running their family business more successfully in due course.

1. Introduction

The family business is among the most important building blocks of a nation's economy and has gradually come under the radar of leading experts and academics. From small and mid-sized organizations to multinational corporations, family-run businesses set high performance standards and bear lessons to be learned for the broader business community. In both mature and emerging countries, family-owned businesses make a substantial contribution to economic development and represent a core base of long-term, sustainable growth. The top league of these businesses is well known family run Business Company such as BMW, Nike, Roche, Tata Group and Walmart these companies are well versed companies in worldwide. In many cases, there is less known family business running are existed in India and served better to the development of the Indian Nation.

In India, the role of family businesses is remarkable one which focuses in nation building, wealth creation, employment generation and contribution to the exchequer. While a few Indian family businesses have followed the same lines of business started by their fathers or grandfathers and grown these significantly, rests have diversified considerably by setting up new businesses, exploring new sectors and markets, expanding geographically, and increasing their global footprint.

From small and medium enterprises to large conglomerates, it is interesting to note that family businesses have contributed to the growth of every sector in India and it always interesting to find out how they are evolved over a period of time, how they perceived their business prospects, what they think they need to do in their business to take it forward for adjusting with changing environment, including dealing with the five mega trends shaping the business world (PWC- Family business Survey 2016).

Diagram I

Diagram II

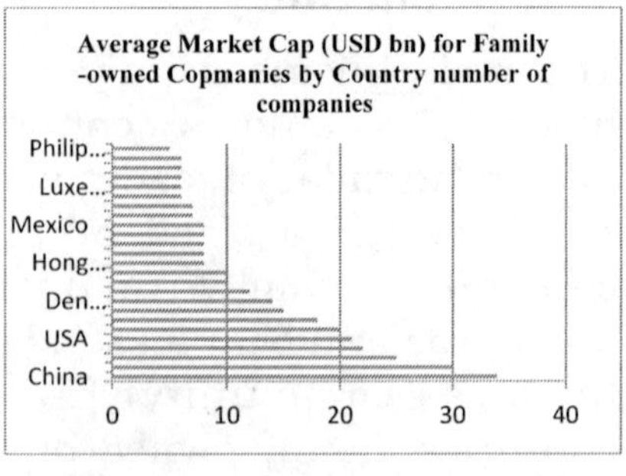

Source: Company data, Credit Suisse estimates

2. Meaning and Definition

Meaning of Family Business: A person starts his/ her business to fulfill the needs of his/ her family. When this business passes from one generation to other is known as family business. Family business is a business governed and /or managed on a sustainable, potentially cross-generational basis to shape and perhaps pursue the formal or implicit vision of the business held by members of the same family or a small number of families.

Donnelly (1964) defined the family firm as one which has been closely identified with at least two generations of a family and when this link has had a mutual influence on company policy and on the interests and objectives of the family.

Chua et al. (1999) in their definition of the family business have pointed out that the family business is governed and/or managed with the intention to shape and pursue the vision of the business held by the members of the family in a manner that is potentially sustainable across generations of the family. Family firms have a complex array of factors that may impact performance outcome of the business. The interaction of the family, individual family members, and the firm, create unique conditions and constituencies that have diverse value propositions and outcome expectations.

European Union (2009) Definition can further enlarge as firm of any size, is a family business run as

- The majority of decision-making rights are in the possession of the natural person(s) who established the firm or in the possession of the natural person(s) who has/have acquired the share capital of the firm or in the possession of their spouses, parents, child or children's direct heirs;
- At least one representative of the family or kin is formally involved in the governance of the firm. Listed companies may meet the definition of a

family business, if the person who founded the company or has acquired the share capital of the company, or their family or descendants, due to their share capital, hold 25 per cent of decision making rights. The definition also includes family businesses that have not yet completed the first generation transfer. It also includes sole proprietors and self-employed if a legal entity exists that can be transferred to the next generation

3. Conceptualization

The family business could regard as the interaction of three distinct systems which are ownership, management and family. Family members often create new firms together; fund new ventures rather than seeking true venture capital. It has also been observed that as exit strategy, entrepreneurs are more likely to pass their firms to their families instead of going public. There are theories on family business; one of the most prominent theories is Three Circle Model theory. This examination of the various systems which makes up the family business of ownership system, the family system and the business system has been another significant area of family business research interest (Holland, 1981; Davis P, 1983; Tagiuri and Davis J, 1982, 1996).

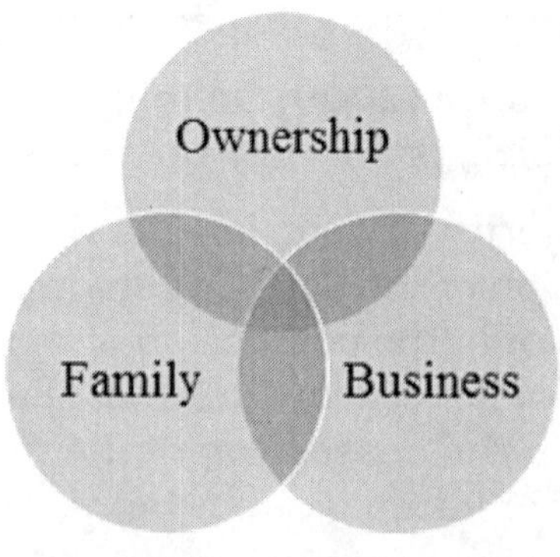

Source: Tagiuri and Davis, (1982) and Tagiuri and Davis (1992:49).

Fig.1: Three Circle Model

As noted by Meredith (1993: 305), unique to any investigation of the family firm, compared to non-family firms, is the fact that in addition to the system of the organization, another whole system is being looked at the family system. There is an influence from members of the family, both those within and those outside the firm. Family to family and family to non-family relationships clearly influence the dynamics of the business.

Family businesses are classified into two types. The first one is the business run by the family members are prime in their business. In the case of second type of business represents the family members and partners which hold by family and controlling power. Family business has significant roles in their business such as family vision strategy and governance, business vision strategy and governance, succession planning, ownership structure, conflict resolution mechanism, preserving wealth, induction and grooming, recruitment and reward of non family professional, retirement and estate planning and compensation and rewards.

4. Research Question

- Does family business exist in India?
- What extent the family business contributes to Indian economy?

5. Objective of the Study

- To explore the existence of family businesses in India and
- To access the contribution of family businesses to Indian economic development.

6. Research Methodology

This is an exploratory study with the collection various secondary data from journals, news papers, published speeches from family business houses, family business survey reports (2014 to 2017). Since it is qualitative study, no statistical tools have been used for this research.

7. Contribution of Family Businesses

The Family businesses enable the Indian economy system by providing employment opportunity to local people in significant level which increase the money flow among the country fellows. In India, family businesses accounted 70 per cent of the total sales and net profits of the biggest 250 private sector companies. The role of business in the society has witnessed a dramatic change in the recent times. It is interesting to note that family business contributes 60 per cent of Gross Domestic Product across the world.

Subsequently, Indian Family Businesses are functioning as 'backbone' to the Indian economy so as need of an hour to extend the life span of the family businesses so that the economy could streamline to derive benefit from its contribution because of in 1947, there were 18 families owned nearly every valuable companies in the country which were controlled by 50 families (Agarwala 2001). India is the fastest growing major economy in the world and a large number of economists and policymakers expect the country's economy to grow by around 7.5 per cent in the financial year ending March 2017. As against this, global growth is expected to be around 3.1 per cent and that of advanced nations, 1.8 per cent in 2016.

It is no wonder, then, that over the next 5 years, Indian family businesses expect to grow steadily (49 per cent) or quickly and aggressively (35 per cent). Thus, business family remains the most powerful and enduring entity in corporate India from its very inception. India's richest business families are: Azim Premji (Wipro); Ambani (Mukesh and Anil) (Reliance Industries); Sunil Mittal (Bharti); Shiv Nadar (HCL); Dilip Sanghvi (Sun Pharma); Birla KM (Hindalco, Grasim...); Bajaj Rahul (Bajaj Auto); Hamied Y K (Cipla); Munjal B (Hero). On October 29, 2007 billionaire Mukesh Ambani became the richest person in the world.

The contribution of family business was high in India in terms of employment and income generation and wealth creation. Several visionaries had established their business ventures at different places of the country and abroad. In India, the big business groups are present in every sector of the economy and "loom large in the Indian mind". In the following, their role as the economy's backbone is quantified. Indian business houses are highly visible in the media, society and economy, this holds for their products and their people. Growing international competition, however, forces them to streamline their businesses. The Indian family business has transformed itself to be competitive on a global scale when it struck during the world recession. Indian family business visionaries are concentrated on six core businesses competencies such as systematically trained employees and installed sophisticated corporate governance structures.

8. Conclusion

In the emerging society, Indian family businesses are an integral part to the economic development of the country. Which shape their nations' economies and contribute immensely in order improve the Gross Domestic Product. India's family business groups or business houses are collections of highly diversified firms that are controlled by a family. Firstly, look back on a rich and successful history were begins in the 18th and 19th century. They have proven unusually robust when faced with major economic and political crises in the 20th century. Secondly, they form the backbone of their respective economies.

A large percentage of Indian businesses, particularly the biggest family run business belong to a family business house. Thirdly, they are traditionally family-owned. But the structure of their characteristic family ownership differs. Both confront similar problems associated with family ownership, for instance accusations of inefficient allocation of resources. Fourthly, they are characterized by trans-generational continuity and long-term orientation which is mostly due to their family ownership. In India, it is characterized by market failures and a soft government that cannot fill the existing institutional and intermediary voids. The business groups are diversified across all the sectors of the industry. Their numerous operations fill the institutional voids left by the weak state and act as a market intermediary. It enables them to exploit entrepreneurial opportunities. Indian business groups have complex and bureaucratic structures. Indian business groups products and leaders are highly visible. Even though there are tremendous cultural, economic and political differences in the countries, one finds that the family businesses are deeply rooted in their respective societies and pursued with passion to contribute their share in welfare and development of the nation.

References

1. Astrakhan J H (1988), 'Family Firm and Community Culture', Family Business Review,1 (2):165-189
2. Baker, Chistopher Jhon (1981), An Indian Rural Economy 1880-1955: The Tamil Nadu Country Side, Oxford University Press, New Delhi.
3. Collins, L O' Regan (2011), 'The Evolving Field of Family Business', Family Business Review, 1 (1): 5-13.
4. Carlock, R., (2007), "Family business on the couch", available at http://knowledge.insead.edu/ family-business/family-values-leading-the-way-out-of-the-downturn-1431
5. Dyer, J W G (2006), 'Examining the Family Effect on Firm Performance', Family Business Review, 19 (4): 253-273.
6. Ernestro J Poza (2010), Family Business, South-Western Publication, Nashville, USA.
7. Florance W Kaslow (2006), Hand Book of Family Business and Consultation: A Global Prespective, Routledge, UK.
8. Gita Priamal, Margaret Herdeck (1986), India's Industrialists, Three Continent Press, Washington, D.C.
9. Javar, R., (2010), Organizational Change: Family Business, Institute of Advanced Management Education and Entrepreneurship (IAMEE), Hyderabad.
10. http://ec.europa.eu/
11. http://publications.creditsuisse.com

2

A Study on Constraints in Tribal Education: With Special Reference to Paniyasin Kerala

— ***Aggi Mary Anto***

Abstract

Education is a key enabler which determines the capability of individuals. This unequivocally determines the freedom of choice to attain the opportunities to improve one's socio-economic condition. The educational advancement is regarded as the main catalyst for social development. Though Paniyas are the largest tribal community in Kerala they pay very little importance to education. Most of them are not yet conscious about the benefits of education and consequent of economic gains and also they believed that the educated young generation is reluctant to take up their traditional occupations.

It is found that the major barrier of illiteracy among the Paniyas which has led them to backwardness in socio-economic abject and also another leading hindrance factor is dropout rate which is exists high among the tribes due to the lack of awareness and tent the negative attitude of parents towards the education of their children. In this context, the present study is an attempt to unveil the hidden constraints in tribal education for increasing tribal school dropouts among the students of tribal groups in Kerala with special reference to the Paniya Tribe. The economic backwardness acts as a road block to education of tribal children so that an hour is needed to find out reality persists in tribal environment and study findings could pave a way to solve the unattended issues exists in Paniya Tribe particularly in education.

Introduction.

In the contemporary environment, education is a powerful instrument for individuals to achieve upward socio-economic mobility and power in the society. The socio-economic growth of a country depends, to a large extent, on the constant growth rate of literacy and availability of skilled and educated man power. Education could conceive as the panacea of all social disparity. In India, everyprogram is planned and implemented successfully according to the growth of social development so as literacy is the key element in order to attain the social improvement at grassroots level of tribal people.

In Kerala, the major tribal communities are Paniyan (44.77%), MulluKuruman (17.51%), Kurichian (17.38%), Kattunaikan (9.93%), Adiyar (7.10%) and UraliKuruman (2.69%). They are categorized in three major types, as agricultural labourers, marginal farmers and forest dependents. Paniyan and Adiyar communities who were traditionally bonded labourers and UraliKuruman, traditionally artisans constitute the major part of agricultural labourers. The Paniyas are the largest scheduled tribe in Kerala among other 36 tribal groups in Kerala in which altogether contribute 22.5% of the total tribal population. They spread over at Wayanad, Kannur, Kozhikode, Malapuaram and Palakkad districts and in some parts of Karnataka and Tamil Nadu states. The overwhelming majority (72%) of the total Paniya population in the state is concentrated in Wayanad district. The tribe are distinctive in anthropological descriptions such as dark in skin, long headed with broad noses, short physique and curly hair.

The language of Paniya tribe is 'Paniya'; a mixture of ancient forms of Malayalam and Tamil which has no script. For any indigenous community, the role of language is not merely limited as a medium of communication rather it conveys the history of their culture and knowledge. The legends, myth, history and struggles are conveyed and transmitted by folk songs and stories through oral communication. Animals, birds, trees, God are becoming the characters of these traditional chants. These traditional songs could see as the strong narrations of their culture and identity. In many songs, they convey several myths about their origin and exploitations experienced in their history. Their struggle against oppression and exploitation is embodied within these songs.

In terms of the schooling of the tribal children is observed that dropout which is one of the major problems prevailing in Kerala. The dropout rate for the Wayanad district in the three stages of schooling (lower primary, upper primary and high school) put together is 6.6%, which is the highest in comparison with all the other districts. For the lower primary school level and upper primary school level, the dropout rate is highest in Wayanad district. However, dropout rate for ST students of Wayanad district at high school level is lower than many other districts. It is very common in the area that most of the parents prefer to stop their children's education in the midway. There are some habitations where the Paniyas did not even think about sending their children for schooling. When the children reach the age of six, they participate in the income earning processes of their household. Boys will go for working as agricultural labourers, and girls will assist in household activities like looking after the infants in the home.

In short, the schooling of children in these communities is so much dependent on the household's decision and child's interest is the underlying causes which thwart them to withdraw. In this scenario, the present study has framed the following major objectives as follow

Objectives of the Study

1. To identify various constraints in the education of the Paniya tribal pupils

2. To offer suggestions to minimize the educational constraints of tribal pupils of Kerala

The present study results has discussed in two major thrust areas such as constraints of the Paniya Tribals pupils in educational aspects and recommendations and suggestions in order resolve the issues which is existed.

Findings of the Study: Constraints in Paniyas Tribal Education

There are many critical issues and problems in the field of tribal education which are

- **New Medium of language** – Language is one of the important constraints of tribal children which prevents them access to education.
- **The Location of the School** - The physical barriers create a hindrance for the children of a tribal village to attend the school in a neighbouring village.
- **Economic Condition** - The abject economic condition of tribal people has made them to hold their children from educational panacea
- **Prevailing Attitude of the parents** - As education does not yield any immediate economic return, the tribal parents prefer to engage their children in remunerative employment which supplements the family income
- **Educational Institutional mismanagement-** In the remote tribal areas the teacher absenteeism is a regular phenomenon which affects largely the quality of education
  - **Lack of Proper monitoring system-** Proper monitoring hindrance and coordination between the Tribal Welfare Department and School Education Department led the tribal students to prefer go for working even in school hours.

- **Prolonged General Amenities Issues:**
  - Tribal pupils are not even having minimum facilities for study at home. Their Poor socio-economic conditions result in irregular attendance, less concentration in studies, failure in the examinations, inhibition in interacting with other students and development of disinterest towards learning.
  - Institutions like libraries, Information Communication Technology centres etc. which would have catered to the education of the tribes are almost nearly absent in tribal belts. At present provisions to watch educational tele-programmes are not available to tribal students.
  - Early marriage of tribal children, especially girls, was found to be a factor adversely affecting the education of the tribal pupils.
  - Drug addiction of tribal parents was found to be adversely affecting the educational interest of tribal children.
  - Many tribal students have to travel long distances sometimes through mid-forests to reach the school and there is a need for more tribal promoters in tribal belts.
  - The tribal pupils are found to be badly in need of private tuition. But they do not have enough financial background to afford paid tuition.
  - The motive of tribal pupils in joining hostel is getting better learning facilities, better food and better living conditions. Density of schools in the tribal belts is found to be very low. This causes difficulties for tribal pupils in attending schools.
  - The study found that in large spectrum day care centres are not available in many of the tribal centres. This causes inconveniences to working

tribal mothers who are forced to depute school going tribal children to look after their younger siblings.

- The prevailing incentives are generally considered inadequate by tribal pupils and parents. Hostel facilities presently available for tribal pupils are quite inadequate. There are no parental incentives at the high school level. Lump-sum-grant and stipend at present given as incentives are inadequate to meet the needs of the tribal pupils.
- Free study tour facilities and free transport facilities are almost non-existent incentives except for tribal hostel inmates. There is a general dissatisfaction about the complimentary incentives on the basis of final examination results and performance in extracurricular activities.
- Inadequate governmental incentives put the tribal students to many hardships such as parents are not able to meet the educational expenses and provide learning facilities, students are forced to work for wages and their interaction with others gets poorer. Sometimes even the discontinuation of their education is the consequence.
- Tribal students are put to a lot of hardships in the absence of free supply of learning materials and free food.
- Many tribal parents generally have still unfavourable attitude towards the education. Most of the tribal parents do not motivate their children to go to school.
- Tribal parents do not usually provide sufficient learning materials for their children. Tribal parents are not in the habit of compelling children to study at home. They are also found

to be reluctant to consult teachers regarding the education of their children and also to attend PTA and MPTA meetings. Unfavourable attitude of parents is also evident in not providing enough additional finance for the education of their children.

- Financial backwardness acts as a strong constraint in the education of the tribal children. Most of the parents are hesitant to spend money from their pockets for the cause of education. Some parents even misappropriate government educational incentives given to their children.
- Lack of parental insistence and study facilities at homes refrains tribal pupils from studying after school hours. Discussion with teachers shows that sizable number of teachers extend considerable help for the education of the tribal pupils. The nature of the help extended include providing additional attention during class hours, peer teaching, motivating parents towards education and stimulating students to take learning more seriously. But free tuition is provided only by a microscopic minority of teachers.
- Majority of teachers confront with difficulties in teaching tribal pupils. The difficulties mainly hail from poor standard of the tribal pupils, their lack of interest towards learning, their irregular attendance and lack of parental support in their learning.
- Teachers are not in receipt of special training for tribal education. Majority of the teachers are interested in getting additional training. The anticipated duration of the training by majority of the teachers is less than 20 days. During the in service programme they expect training for motivating tribal pupils, instructional strategies

suitable for tribal pupils including their psychology and some training in tribal dialect.

- Tribal students and parents believe that absence of additional help from teachers will have unfavourable impact upon the education of tribal pupils. Social workers and teachers also endorse the view. The main possible consequences include securing poor marks in examinations, becoming lazy in studies, inability to compete with non- tribal students, irregular attendance and less participation in co-curricular activities.
- Tribal pupils, social workers and educational experts anticipate further additional help from the teaching community. They want the present help extended to be provided on a larger scale. It is also desired to arrange remedial teaching for tribal pupils, identify their talents and organize suitable co-curricular activities and motivate them for higher studies.
- Academic constraints exist in the education of tribal pupils. The reasons for this generally are that they have to study many things not quite useful for their future, matters taught are unrelated to life situation, difficulty in understanding text book language and compulsion to study matters against conventional beliefs.
- There are inadequacies in the available school facilities. The inadequacies are conspicuous in laboratories, libraries, furniture, buildings and playground. Improvement in school facilities will result in the improvement of learning by tribal pupils.
- The improvement in school facilities will be conspicuous in the areas of securing more marks in examinations, stimulation of interest

towards education and participation in co-curricular activities.

Suggestions for Improvement of Tribal Students' Education

The study is an attempt to offer its suggestions for resolving the existing issues. The following suggestions could carry out to ensure the tribal students' education at grassroots level and welfare of them.

- **Conduction of literacy campaign** - Proper awareness campaign should be organized to create the adequate awareness about the importance of education among the tribal. Extensive literacy campaign in the tribal dominated districts may be undertaken on a priority basis to literate the tribal.
- **Changing the attitude of the tribal parents** - The attitude of the tribal parents toward education should be improved through proper counselling and guidance.
- **Ready-reckon in relevant study materials in local languages** - All study materials should be supplied in local languages of tribes.
- **Make arrangement for appointment of Local teachers** - It is suggested to appoint more tribal teachers and female teachers in the tribal areas. The ecological, cultural, psychological characteristics of tribal children should be considered carefully by the teachers in tribal areas.
- **Providing sufficient stipends and scholarships** - Since higher education among the tribes is less, special ST scholarships should be provided to the tribal students perusing higher education, particularly in medical, engineering, and other vocational streams.
- **Establishment of residential schools** - More residential schools should be established in each

states and districts and extended up to Post Graduate level in tribal areas.

- **Ensuring the social security**- Social security of students, especially of adolescent girls is of great concern in residential schools.
- **Implement proper monitoring** - Higher level officials should check the functioning of schools frequently relating to the teaching methods, working hours, and attendance registers.

Conclusion

The education is the key factor to the welfare and development of tribal people. The tribal children have very low levels of participation in educational environment. It is observed that though the development of the tribes is taking place in India but the pace of development has been rather slow so as government should take concrete steps for the welfare and development of tribal education by enabling the basic amenities in tribal areas at war foot basis and also public support is very much essential to improve the educational standards in tribal area and also should arrange adequate employment opportunities for the tribal to get better economic upliftment in order change the perspective of educational as a boon for their sustainable welfare and development.

References

1. Aerthayil Mathew, *Impact of Globalisation on Tribals in the context of Kerala*, Rawat Publications, New Delhi, 2008.
2. Bagai Sweta and Nundy Neera, *Tribal Education- A Fine Balance*, Rakesh Press, New Delhi, 2009.
3. Devendra Thakur and DN Thakur, *Tribal Life in India-Tribal Life and Forests*, ISBN 978- 81-8450-104-9, New Elegant Printers, New Delhi, 2009.
4. Dropouts 2007-2012, Office of the deputy Director of Education, Wayanad, Kerala, 2013.
5. Mathur P.R.G, *Encyclopaedia of Dravidian Tribes*, International School of Dravidian Linguistics, Thiruvananthapuram,1996.

6. Planning Commission Report, India Vision 2020, Government of India (2002)
7. Venugopal. M, *Adivasiyude Neethinyayam*, Vol. 15, 2018.
8. Working group report of the development of education of SC/ST/ Minorities/Girls and other disadvantaged groups for11th five-year plan (2007-2012), Planning Commission, Govt. of India, (2007)
9. http://www.edutopia.org (2014)

3

Functions of Local Self Government in Infrastructure Development with Respect to Women

— ***Kabilan. I.V***

Abstract

The rural development is a vital factor for efficient governance which focuses welfare and development at grassroots level. The rural livelihood depends upon the effective administration which ensures the speedy development so as the Government of India and State Governments have made concrete steps to implement the various development schemes at village level with the support of Local Governance. In this background, the present study is an attempt to find out the functions of Local Self Government with a special emphasis on women welfare and development in Thirupporur Village.

Introduction

Rural development is the process of improving the life style pattern and economic security of people at grassroots level. Rural development has traditionally positioned on the exploitation of land-intensive natural resources such as agriculture and forestry. However, changes in global production networks and increased growth have made changes in the character of rural areas. Increasingly leisure industry, role manufacturers, and restoration have replaced the resources which extraction led the agriculture as dominant economic drivers[1]. The need for rural populations to approach expansion from a wider perspective so as it has created more focus on a broad range of development goals rather than generating incentive for agricultural and resource-based facilities.

In order to improve the rural areas, the education, entrepreneurship, physical infrastructure, and social infrastructure are needed to streamline and also strengthened for its sustainable development. It is also significant that rural governance has characterized by its emphasis on locally produced economic development strategies.[2] In contrast to urban regions, which have many parallels, rural areas are highly distinctive from one another for this reason, there is a wide range of approaches have adopted. Rural development is inclusiveness in nature.

It fundamentally focuses on action for the development of areas outside the typical urban economic system so as decide what type of rural development is needed in course with the rapid transformation of villages which leads to urbanization that could affect the purview of village environment[3].

Local Self Government in India: A Glance

The Local Self-Government in India refers to administrative jurisdictions below the level of the state. India is a centralized republic with three domains of government: Central (Union), State and Local. The 73rd and 74th constitutional amendments provide acknowledgement and protection to local governments and in addition each state has its own local government legislation. Since 1993, local regime in India takes place in two very distinct forms. Urban localities, covered in the 74th amendment to the Constitution but derive their powers from the individual state governments, while the powers of rural localities have been formalized under the ***Panchayati Raj*** system, under the 73rd amendment to the Constitution. For the history of traditional local government in India and South Asia.

This has added a new Part-IX to the Constitution of India. It is entitled as 'The Panchayats' and consists of provisions from Articles 243 to 243. In addition, the Act has also added a new Eleventh Schedule to the Constitution. This Schedule contains 29 fundamental items of the Panchayats. It deals with Article 232-G. The act is a significant landmark in the evolution of grassroots democratic institutions in the country. It transfers the representative democracy into participatory democracy. It is a revolutionary concept to build democracy at the grassroots level in the country.

The Act provides for the reservation of not less than one-third of the total number of seats for women (including the number of seats reserved for the SCs and STs). Further not less than one-third of the total number of offices of chairpersons in the Panchayats at each level shall be reserved for women. This has rotated among different Panchayats at each level. The Act also authorizes the legislature of a state to make any provision for reservation of seats in any Panchayat and offices of chairperson in the Panchayat at any level in favour of backward classes.

As of recent data in 2017, there are a total of 267,428 local government bodies of which 262,771 are rural and 4,657 urban[4]. Of the rural local governments, 632 are zila parishad at the district level, 6,672 are panchayat samaiti at the block level, and 255,466 are gram panchayat at the village level. Following the 2013 Local election 37.1% of councilors were women[5], and in 2015/16 local government expenditure was 16.3% of total government expenditure

Functions of Local Self Government

The Local Self-Governments are those bodies that safeguard the administration of a subject and a small group equivalent to the village. These bodies are appointed by using the government representing the local inhabitants, which raises its earnings partly through regional taxation an extra manner. The Local Self-Government has divided into institutions, Cities and Municipalities[6].

The Local Self-Governance laws are legislated for the decentralization and democratization of governance within the country together with the enhancement of the contribution of everyone and the institutional development of Local bodies to undergo the accountability for undertaking plans on the locality stage. These laws are constituted the progress of the self-governance process in a fashion for local bodies to surge leadership and make choices on issues affecting them and the lives of the persons and for the development of Village development Committees[7] which play a huge meaning in mission implementation and monitoring on the local degree.

There are a few basic features and functions of the local self-government in India. Those functions stand as pillars for the development

(a) Devolution of such powers, responsibilities, and means and resources as are required to make the local bodies well performing in local self-governance.
(b) Building and progress of institutional[8] mechanism and functional composition in local bodies in a position of for the reason that for neighborhood humans and demeanor obligations.
(c) Devolution of powers to collect and activate such approach and resources as are required to discharge the functions, obligations, responsibility and accountability conferred to the local bodies.
(d) Having the local bodies oriented closer to beginning the civil society established[9] on the democratic process, apparently follow, public accountability, and kinsmen and women's participation, in conducting the features devolved on them.

Review of Literature

An Evaluation of Private Sector Provision of Public Infrastructure in Australian Local Government[10] by John Cannadi analysed that Private region provision of public infrastructure in Australia in any respect degrees of government, including local authorities, has steadily expanded over the last twenty years. Nevertheless, this method of providing public infrastructure remains debatable.

Government Spending, Growth and Poverty in Rural India by Schengen Fan Peter Hazell and Sukhadeo Thora[11] wrote that Using kingdom-level information for 1970–ninety-three, a simultaneous equation model changed into evolved to estimate the direct and oblique outcomes of different styles of government expenditure on rural poverty and productivity increase in India.

The results show that with the intention to reduce rural poverty, the Indian government must deliver highest priority to additional investments in rural roads and agricultural research.

Objectives

This research is based on the very objective of proving the aforesaid functions of local self-government in practical nature. This study is aimed to check whether the functions of local self-government are correctly executed or not.

Methodology

The methodology the study takes aid from is non empirical sources. The study relies upon sources which are available from internet, books, statutes, census reports and other indirect data collection ideologies.

Analysis and interpretation

The analysis of this study is based on the demarcation of Thiruporur village. The data collected through the census and analyzed the functioning of the LSG in Thiruporur.

According to the census Thiruporur is a Town Panchayat city in district of Kancheepuram, Tamil Nadu. The Thiruporur city is distributed into 15 wards for which elections are held every 5 years. The Thiruporur Town Panchayat has population of 13,666 of which 7,028 are males while 6,638 are females as per report released by Census India 2011. Population of Children with age of 0-6 is 1552 which is 11.36 % of total population of Thiruporur (TP). In Thiruporur Town Panchayat, Female Sex Ratio is of 945 against state average of 996. Moreover, Child Sex Ratio in Thiruporur is around 1003 compared to Tamil Nadu state average of 943. Literacy rate of Thiruporur city is 84.52 % higher than state average of 80.09 %. In Thiruporur, Male literacy is around 90.60 % while female literacy rate is 78.04 %. Thiruporur Town Panchayat has total supervision over 3,256 houses to which it supplies basic amenities like water and sewerage. It is also approved to form roads within Town Panchayat limits and levy taxes on properties coming under its jurisdiction.

This has added a new Part-IX to the Constitution of India. It is entitled as 'The Panchayats' and consists of provisions from Articles 243 to 243. In addition, the Act has also added a new Eleventh Schedule to the Constitution. This Schedule contains 29 fundamental items of the Panchayats. It deals with Article 232-G. The act is a significant landmark in the evolution of grassroots democratic institutions in the country.

It transfers the representative democracy into participatory democracy. It is a revolutionary concept to build democracy at the grassroots level in the country. The Act provides for the reservation of not less than one-third of the total number of seats for women (including the number of seats reserved for the SCs and STs). Further not less than one-third of the total number of offices of chairpersons in the Panchayats at each level shall be reserved for women. This would be rotated among different

Panchayats at each level. The Act also authorises the legislature of a state to make any provision for reservation of seats in any Panchayat or offices of chairperson in the Panchayat at any level in favour of backward classes. Out of over-all population, 4,640 were affianced in work or business activity. Of this 3,543 were males while 1,097 were females. In census survey[12], worker is defined as person who does business, job, service, and cultivator and labour activity. Of total 4640 working population, 86.94 % were engaged in Main Work while 13.06 % of total workers were engaged in Marginal Work.

The Town panchayat over these years have done major functions to the development of Thiruporur, over these years. The main emphasis was laid to educational developments[13].

- Monthly Review meeting for teachers
- Exposure visits for teachers.
- Training for teachers camp viz maths camp at Hyderabad, Activity based training camp at Thiruporur, child care training camp at Thiruporur.

Celebration of World women's day programme on March 8th with the participation of NGOs and women of migrated families

The outcome of those activities were

Teachers improved presentation of subjects

- 75 percent level of party is reached and New plans of monitoring the students' progress are introduced by the teachers.

World women's day programme was organised with the support of the Gender Justice Forum, Tamil Nadu.

- 173 migrated women participated in the programme. Women's awareness regarding their rights and status of their positions has been developed.

- The benefits received through the implementation of the programmes are widespread
- Literacy and skills were improved.
- Students who had discontinued and lost their studying opportunities are able to continue their education.
- Free books, uniforms, noon-meal and writing materials have been provided.
- Free nutritious food for the babies in the day-care centres.
- Offered medical check-up and free medicines and nutritious tonics.
- Gained practical knowledge about animals, birds and reptiles in the zoo and crocodile park about sky, earth, planets and starts at Birla Planetarium and historical knowledge in the antique museum situated in Chennai City.
- Awareness regarding women's rights.
- Food and shelter at residential hostel.

V. Summary of the gender wise disaggregated beneficiaries[14].

Programmes	Beneficiaries		Total number of beneficiaries
	Female	Male	
School curriculum activities	95	91	186 (Children between 6 to 14 age)
Day-care centre	72	75	147 (Babies below 6 years)
Residential training programme	28	29	57 students
Residential hostel	00	11	11 Students
Counselling, intractions and women's day programmes	568	237	805
Total	763	443	1206

Conclusion

From the above analysis it is been found out that the functions of local self -government is being well carried out in Thiruporur Village. The Town Panchayats were conferred with individual administrative powers and unique functional characters have been in existence for over a century. The Town Panchayats adopt well devised accounting and auditing procedures and the service delivery to the public has been better. Town Panchayats are under the administrative control Municipal Administration and Water Supply Department, at Govt. level. The Town Panchayats are places of importance such as Division / Taluk headquarters, Tourist Spots, Pilgrim Centres and Commercial/Industrial towns. This has necessitated special attention to the civic needs of the Town Panchayats. They focus more on education compared to other developments. A suggestion would be on improving the other areas also so that an efficient rural system is established.

Notes

1. Rural Governance available at https://journals.openedition.org/echogeo/15265 last viewed at 05/01/2019
2. edepot.wur.nl/16322
3. sk.sagepub.com/books/rural-geography/n11.xml
4. Van Assche, K. and Hornidge, A. (n.d.). *Rural development.*
5. Kvartiuk, V. (2015). *Participatory governance in rural development.* Halle (Saale): Leibniz-InstitutfurAgrarentwicklung in Transformationsokonomien (IAMO).
6. Røiseland, A. (2010). Local self-government or local co-governance? *Lex localis - Journal of Local Self-Government,* 8(2), pp. 133-145.
7. Functions of local self- government available at https://brainly.in/question/2578166 last viewed at 05/01/2019
8. Meaning and functions of Local Self-government at www.publishyourarticles.net last viewed on 05/01/2019
9. Role of self-government https://lexquest.in/role-of-local-self-governmentlast viewed on 05/01/2019
10. John Cannadi An Evaluation of Private Sector Provision of Public Infrastructure in Australian Local Government Volume 82, Issue 4 November 2000 Published at Australian Economic Review.
11. Vidhee Kiran Avashia, Amit GargUrban Infrastructure and Governance Mission under JNNURM Vol. 51, Issue No. 2, 09 Jan, 2016
12. Wisdom Jobs. (2019). *CENSUS AND SAMPLE SURVEY in Research Methodology - CENSUS AND SAMPLE SURVEY in Research Methodology (11466) | Wisdom Jobs.* [online] Available at: https:/

/www.wisdomjobs.com/e-university/research-methodology-tutorial-355/census-and-sample-survey-11466.html [Accessed 21 Jan. 2019].

13. Town Panchayat. (2019). *Rural Development.* [online] Available at: http://www.rdttrust.com/ [Accessed 21 Jan. 2019].
14. Town Panchayat. (2019). *Rural Development.* Available at: http://www.rdttrust.com/ [Accessed 21 Jan. 2019].

4

Re-ordering the Ordained: The Role of Organized Priestly Training of the Syrian Catholic Community in the Social Formation and the Upliftment of the Weaker Sections of Kerala

— Ajesh George

Introduction

India is a land of diversities which are religion, class, caste, language, culture, affinities, anthropological and peculiarities. The Religion plays an important role in the welfare and development at grassroots level. It is understood that India is a land of religions, faith and the people are led by the instructions and prescriptions of the priestly class. Priest[1] also assumes the position of the leader of the community."[2] The role of the priest in every religious community was varying according to socio political and ecclesial dimensions of the life of the community. In the initial days of the Christian community the priest was mainly taking care of the liturgical[3] activities of the community. At present scenario, priestly class has become a very important and influential group in the society in determining the social, political, economic, cultural and ecclesial plights of the community. The present study is taken up to understand the transformation occurred to the traditional Thomas[4] Christian community of Malabar after the establishment of organized and centralized seminaries[5]. The study has presented with historical analysis of the priestly formation from the pre-Diamper period onwards and the effect of it in the social, political, cultural and economic organization of the society.

A Brief sketch of the priestly formation in the Malabar community: the origin of Christianity in India has very diverse opinions among the historians. There are different traditions such as Thomas tradition, Chaldean Tradition, Bartholomew tradition and so on.

The General Situation of the Clergy among the Christians of Malabar

The church of Thomas Christians was receiving bishops from the Church of East-Syria these priests were known as Cathenars or Casanars which was a Malabarization of the Syriac word *qasisa* and the clerics below the priests grade, whether deacons or not were known as Chemas.[6] Outside the church the priests were not very different from the laymen in their dress. There is no doubt that the priests were generally married. Father M. Carneiro S.J and his companions who had been to the Serra on a visit found that the Cathenars were married and an old Cathenar who was very erudite in scriptures and had taught at the University of Angamaly for fifty years, told the Portuguese.

Priestly Training among the Thomas Christians

The St. Thomas Christians of Malabar were also having almost the same system of priestly formation in the early period of the Church. Young clerics stayed with their masters, who were holy and wise, officially recognized as Malpans. They cut a fatherly figure for the candidates only very scanty information about the Malpanates and their training system before the arrival of the Portuguese. Fr. Thomas Puthiakunnel has attempted to put together the available historical references in his book Syro-Malabar Clergy and their General Obligations.[7] Mgr. Raphael Thattil has tried to develop it further in his work Priestly Formation in the Syro-Malabar Church.[8] The system of priestly formation existed here was the Malpanate system.

Malpanates in Malabar

The system followed for the training of the priests was the Malpanate system. The term Malpan comes from the Syriac term '*Malpana*' which means master or professor. Malpan is a priest who is known for his learning. He is considered as Guru, officially approved and appointed by the Church, as a qualified person to impart an effective priestly formation to his disciples.[9] A candidate to priesthood had to undergo basic education with a guru before he came to a Malpanate for clerical training. The model life and experiential knowledge of Malpans were espoused to the candidates. This kind of encounter with Guru formed a sense of worship, life of sacraments and way of tradition etc. Malpans were highly esteemed and honoured by St.Thomas Christians and exercised great influence in ecclesiastical affairs. The major areas of study were the sacred scripture, canons of the church, Liturgy, Syriac Language etc. The main content of the priestly formation have summed up into few words: The competence in sacred scripture, ability to preach and teach the content of Divine revelation, Celebration of the sacred mysteries and the pastoral care. St. Thomas Christians considered their priests primarily as the ministers of the word of God and worship, and not as the administrators. The administrative role of the clergy was less and they had more time for their priestly ministry as demanded by the community.[10]

Emergence of Seminaries under the leadership of different Congregations and societies

With the arrival of Portuguese to India by the end of the 15th century a new epoch was opened in the history of

Malabar Church. The Malabar Christians welcomed them and hosted them as brethrens of same faith. The Portuguese too had a feeling of affection and trust on St. Thomas Christians and on their liturgy. The presence of Chaldean Bishops and the use of Syriac language in the liturgical ceremonies made serious doubt on Malabar Christians. Though the Portuguese Christians felt happy about the Christian presence but the practices of them annoyed the Portuguese. So they began to interfere in the priestly formation. They established seminaries for the training and some of which were as follows.

- Kodungallor Seminary of Fr. Vicente de Lagos
- Vaippicotta Seminary
- Kaduthuruthy seminary
- Ambazhakkad seminary
- Varapuzha - Alengadu Seminary
- Malpan Seminaries
- Malpan Seminary at Kumarakom (1781)
- Malpan Seminary at Pallipuram
- Mannanam Malpanate
- Mangalapuzha (Padroado) Seminary
- Mannanam Seminary

General Nature of the Formation in those Seminaries

The different seminaries established under the leadership of different congregations and native leadership played a prominent role in the seminary formation. The foreign missionaries reached into a conclusion that the Christianity existing in India is under superstition and to reform them is the duty. So the entire formation system was designed with such a spirit of rectifying the Indian Christianity. They were mainly taught the sacred scripture, principles of faith; moral casus, liturgy and the Syriac language which is the liturgical language of the Malabar Christians were not given importance. The formation the candidates received did not appealing to the needs of the local Christianity. Since those seminaries were not under the control of the local authorities of the Thomas Christians they were hesitant to ordain the candidates coming out from those seminaries.

Puthenpally Seminary- A centralized apparatus of priestly formation

The establishment of Puthenpally Centralized and Apostolic seminary initiated a new process in the development. Along with it the larger process of priestly formation entered into an important and significant phase.

Puthenpally Seminary the First Central Apostolic Seminary

In the year of 1854 Mgr. Bernardine O.C.D, the then Vicar Apostolic of Veraploy laid the corner stone of a pretty big building at Puthenpally. Mgr. Bernadine, the good shepherd painfully noticed that the wounds suffered by his beloved flock were very deep. So this situation insisted him to find out a solution to prevent schismatic teachings. He thought that most efficient means to ward off the evil formed a body of zealous and well educated indigenous priests, loyal to the religion and pastors. He entrusted his plans to Fr. Marcellinus OCD in 1866, and as its rector, it remained with him to carry out the project. He declared the seminary opened in August 1866. On the 15th of the same month, arrived a little band of four aspirants from Mannanam, where a petit seminary for the Syrians existed at this period they joined by their Latin Confreres.

Academic Life of Puthenpally Seminary[11]

The Seminary of Puthenpally has ever followed a brilliant programme in Ecclesiastical studies. It form a vague idea of the strenuous efforts of the authorities of the seminary had to make, if note that Latin was not formally taught in the seminaries that existed prior to the year 1866. Consequently when they were closed in the course of years and the seminarists came over here; the professors had to undergo various difficulties. For their benefits some of the professors took to themselves with great patience, the heavy burden of translating into Malayalam, Philosophy and Dogmatic Theology, Moral Theology and Ecclesiastical History. The first year the candidate studies Latin language, English, Rhetoric, Profane History and other subjects which were the requisites of advanced ecclesiastical studies. On the remaining 6 years two were to be allotted to the study of Philosophy, including History of the True religion, Latin Poetry and exercises of Syriac and English languages; and the other four years were to be spent on Dogmatic and Moral Theology, Sacred Scripture, Ecclesiastical History, Oratory, Liturgy, Gregorian Chant, Catechism, Moral Classes; besides these the students were to hold academicals debates and the literary meetings very frequently. They were trained in English as well as Syriac too. But the importance of Malayalam was not undermined. The seminary became under the direct control of Propaganda Fide[12] Rome. The Holy See reformed its rules, regulations and programme of studies Under the existing regulations, the course extends over a period of 7 years of which one year is assigned for Rhetoric, two for philosophy and the remaining four years for theology, fundamentals, dogmatic, Moral and pastoral; while the study of Syriac language and liturgy is promoted by having for it set hours every day.

The Socio-Cultural and Ecclesiastical Implications of the Formation at Puthenpally Seminary

The candidates for priesthood received in the Puthenpally Seminary became instrumental in shaping the community in general, compare the formation given to the clergy before the establishment of the Puthenpally seminary with that of later easily trace out lot of differences. The formation was more of social in the sense that candidates were equipped to participate actively in the problems of the society. The various social causes they have been undertaking especially in the beginning of 20th century and in the end decades of 19th century is a great witness to it. In this context, social and Cultural background of the society has discussed for the understanding.

Socio Cultural background of the 20th century Kerala

Kerala society in the beginning of the 20th century was a caste ridden society. The social evils of untouchability, discrimination, caste distinctions and slavery existing only the high class people were allowed to have education and all the social facilities. The people who belong to the lower caste communities were compelled to work for the high class people. The social mobility was also not much because of that, generations of lower class people were subject to poverty and other social problems. People were stratified on the basis of caste, colour, religion and economic parameters which created great social contentment in the society. Culturally speaking Kerala was a land which was embracing the cultural varieties coming from different parts.

All the important social movements in Kerala was happened during those days such as Vaikkom Satyagraha, Guruvayoor Satyagrha, Punnapra Vayalar uprisings, Peasant Uprisings, Mappila Uprisings etc were the major ones. All these social awakenings were taking part of the development of the social life of the Kerala Society. The Ezhava Memorial, Nair Memorial Malayalee Memorial, Abstention movement etc were examples of caste organizations and associations. The people of Kerala in the beginning of the 20th century were gathered under the name of their caste and were fighting for their rights. So community mobilization and organization was also very strong during those days. The different organizations and associations in the context of the nationalist movement actually made the background for the community mobilization.

The Changing Nature of Priest and his Changing Role in the Society.

In the 20th century one of the major changes observed in the life of the church was the changing nature of the priests and their role in the church as well as in the society. Till the end of the 19th century the major role of the priest was similar to that of a *Poojari* in the temple, as just officiate the liturgical functions, read the sacred scripture, interpret it to the people. "The priests who received formal training in the seminaries established in those days became leaders in the community. They were organizing the ecclesial communities as well as the community in general. A radical transformation in the nature of the priests by the beginning of 20th century, though the priests were there from the very beginning, but this radical shift happened to them was caused by the systematic and organized training which they received from the seminaries especially from the Puthenpally Seminary the first central apostolic seminary in Kerala."[13] The fact is that there was a radical change in the nature of the priests in the beginning of the 20th century. There was a changing in the nature of the priest from mere a cultic priest to one who is leading and molding the community.

The Ecclesial Impacts of the Priestly Training

The seminary formation has very clear impacts on the society

Moral Disciplining

One of the major areas of importance and care was that of Moral disciplining. The priests consider themselves as the custodians of morality. When we analyze the curriculum of the Puthenpally Seminary the major importance was given to the moral teaching.[14] There were number of hours set aside for the teaching of morality. Even in the evenings they were gathered and discussed about the Moral discourses. The whole training system was communicating the idea that you are going to be the custodians of the morality of the community. The number of pamphlets published from the Puthenpally seminary, in order to give moral education to the community namely[15]

1. Discourses on Marriage
2. Discourses on Confession
3. How to make good confession
4. The Mortal sins
5. The mortal sin and confession
6. Body- The divine gift of God
7. Human Sexuality

An analysis of the *Nalagamams* (Chronicles) of few old parish churches reveals that the priests were giving moral instructions to them at proper times. In the chronicles they have recorded that there were special sermons[16] on moral issues. They considered it as the most important duty of the priest.

Teaching of Catechism

It is in the 20th century the official catechism classes begun among the Syrian Catholic community which was an outcome of the proper seminary training. The catechism classes were mainly for the transmission of basic faith and ideals of faith. In the Nalagamam of the Mylacombu Church was felt to Syrian Catholic Church. It is understood that and the *vedopadesam* classes in church is also felt to Syrian Catholic Church. The classes are mainly arranged for the children from the age of 5 to 15. The world is filled with evil spirit and to prevent our children and the generation from it teaching catechism to the students."[17]

Crystallization of Syrian Identity

Though the Puthenpally Seminary was inter ritual seminary, it helped a lot in making people more conscious about their own rite and Christian identity. This community identity later on helped them to organize themselves to fight for certain rights of them. In the 1920's and 30's the Christians community is getting organized and take the lead of the abstention movement and fighting for their rights. In developing this consciousness the role of priests is very important because priests the leaders of the Christian community actually helped the people to organize themselves and to be authentic Christians. The Curriculum in the seminary was also discussing about the Christian identity consciousness and the growth of it.

The Social impacts of the Priestly training: Upliftment of the weaker sections of the society

The nature of the Kerala society in the 19th and 20th century was not one of equality and equity. A great number of the people were denied of their basic rights and was marginalized in the name of religion and caste. The evils of caste system were very rampant in the Kerala society and that made the life of many people very problematic. It is the Christians who came forward for the first time in the history of Kerala to uplift those weaker sections. Initially the attempt came from the foreign Christian missionaries. But later on when the leadership of the Christian community existed which was transferred to the indigenous Christians they came in the forefront of strengthening the weaker sections. The major affected communities were the people who belonged to the lower strata of the caste system such as scheduled castes, tribes, other backward communities and especially the women. The discrimination was not only in the name of religion alone rather the whole women folk in the community were also facing lot of challenges. The major problems they were facing are given below.

1. The problem of the untouchability for the lower caste
2. They denied the freedom to use the public wells, roads and other public services.
3. They denied permission to enter into the temples.

4. They lacked freedom in dressing up properly.
5. They denied admissions in government schools
6. People were not allowed to learn Sanskrit and the Vedas.
7. No facilities for women education and social upliftment.
8. Denied of medical care or not in a position to approach the existing medical facilities.
9. Social mobility was based purely on religion and no any other merit matters.
10. Social status of them was miserable and the upper caste people even did not consider them as human beings of equal status.

The role of Christian community especially under the leadership of the clergy in bringing social transformation is really commendable especially the social upliftment of the weaker sections of the society.

Educational Initiatives

The only panacea for all the problems was to give proper education to them. The public education system was set apart for the upper caste people. Catholic Church under the auspicious leadership of the priests had begun an educational revolution which triggered the social upliftment of the lower castes. When St. Chavara Kuriackose Elias was the Vicar general he instructed all the priests to establish educational institutions. The formation that the priests received in the centralized Puthenpally Seminary was actually encouraging them to start educational institutions. They were given the conviction that only through education transform the communities and duty. 'The salvific mission of Jesus Christ which need to be followed in life is not for any particular group of people rather it is a universal as well as cosmic salvation. Nobody should be sidelined from acquiring the effects of the same' basing on this conviction lot of educational institutions were begun in different parts of the Kerala along with the parish churches. The priests who studied in the centralized seminaries were lucky to have good education and so they were very particular in promoting the education and the establishment of educational institution. A general survey of the educational institutions begun in the years from 1880 to 1940.

Year	*Number of Educational Institutions*
1880-1890	60
1890-1900	100
1900-1910	150
1910-1920	190
1920-1930	230
1930-1940	250
1940-1950	290

Decennial progress in the number educational institutions[18]

By analyzing this chart understood that there was a gradual increase in the number of educational institutions. Majority of these institutions were begun under the leadership of priests and the parishes. The priests who had already the chance of getting good education were involved in the education process. So they took the leadership of establishing educational institutions to give education to the people. The Sanskrit schools established by them.

Education of Women

Another important community which was in the lower position was the women. Education of the women was another area of importance given by the priests. As a result of that number of women schools were established in the state of Kerala. "The role of Syrian catholic community in educating the women folk of the Kerala society cannot be ignored. Along with giving formal education to the girls, the priests and religious sisters were very particular in preparing them to the family life."[19]

Medical Services

The Christian service rendered to the public especially to the poor and weaker sections were is the medical field. The priests who were filled with missionary zeal began to go to the remotest areas and established dispensaries. The backward people both economically and geographically were not able to approach any of the medical centers of those days. The dispensaries and the health care centers established during those days were a great help to them. The priests who were sent from the seminary with the message of the God, the healer went beyond the geographical territories and established hospitals and dispensaries. The institutions established especially in the Malabar area as well as the tribal areas were of great use. The mission hospitals of Catholic Church actually imbibed the real spirit of the service for the poor. Treatment was given freely to the people and also food was also given to them.

Charity activities

The leadership of the priests in uplifting the weaker sections of the society was commendable. The various social service agencies started under the leadership of the Catholic Church was actually a great driving force in uplifting the weaker sections. The major programme introduced by them were as follows

- Distribution of food grains especially with the help of the foreign nations
- Distribution of clothes and other daily usable things
- Organization of institutions similar to the self help groups
- They were trained in life skills and qualities required for normal human life.
- Priests gave leadership during the time of natural calamities and other problems

- Prevention from the epidemics was another important aspect of service.

All the charity activities were taking place under the leadership of the priests and which were not set apart for the Christians alone rather people of all religion, caste and class were included in that.

Protest movements

In different parts of karalla the protest against the suppression of the backward communities was lead by the priestly class. When we study the history of Kerala which is understood that the role of the priests in organizing and leading the protest. Many of the strikes of the Adivasi groups in various parts of the Kerala were a best example of it.

Conclusion

The study was trying to attempt a wide variety of topics ranging from the history of priestly formation the changes that have happened during the course of events. The impacts of the changes in the method of formation in the ecclesiastical as well as the social political engagements of the priestly community are discussed that how because of the systematic formation and training they become real pastors, social activists and socially committed people. The Re-Ordering of the Ordained was not a single layered process rather it was a multi layered one. The centralized priestly formation centered in Puthenpally seminary actually molded the priest to be the leaders of the community, the builders of the community, and the social reformers in the society. The upliftment of the weaker sections in the society became a major concern of them which was resulted from the understanding of the social nature of the religion. When take the Kerala society, the role of Christians especially of Syrian Christians under the leadership of their priests cannot be ignored. But unfortunately today the so called renaissance leaders and the caste organizations of today are undermining it and trying to boast themselves. That is actually a great harm done to the whole process of historical reconstruction.

Bibiliography

1. A.C.O, Vol. 20, Ref 29/1897 Report of Boniface on the Curriculam Followed in the Seminary. (Cited in the Appendix of 'Syrian Church of India and Her Quest for Autochthonous Bishops', Kottayam: OIRSI, 1995.
2. A.C.O., Collegio Seminarii 1888-1907, Vol 3, protocol R.O.N 2339/ 8 Zaleski on July 3. 1894 (cited in the Appendix of ' Syrian Church of India and Her Quest for Autochthonous Bishops', Kottayam: OIRSI, 1995.
3. A.C.O., ACTA 1889, Vol. 20, F 78 as cited in Cherian Varicattu, The Suriani Church of India, Kottayam: OIRSI, 1995.
4. A.C.O., ACTA 1889, Vol. 20, ff, Letter Naratting the General situation of the education and priestly formation (cited in the Appendix of 'Syrian Church of India and Her Quest for Autochthonous Bishops', Kottayam: OIRSI, 1995.
5. ACO, ACTA 1889, vol.20, f.78. (the document is cited in the appendix of; Thomas Kuriakose, Collection of Letters from Malabar to Rome, Pune, JDV 2004)

Secondary Sources- Books, Articles and Unpublished Dissertations

1. Agur C.M, Church History of Travancore, New Delhi: Asian Educational Services, 1990.
2. Anathil George, Theological Formation in India, Poona: Pontifical Athenaeum, 1996.
3. Appassery George, Priestly Formation: Historical and Theological Reflections from an Indian Perspective, Satna: Ephrem Publications, 2010.
4. Ayyer L. Ananthakrishna, Anthropology of the Syrian Christians, Ernakulam...1926,
5. Bernard of St. Thomas, A Brief Sketch of the History of the St. Thomas Christians, Trichinopoly: St. Joseph's Publications, 1924.
6. Brown. L.W, The Indian Christians of St. Thomas: An Account of the Ancient Syrian Church of Malabar, Cambridge: Cambridge University Press, 1956.
7. Charter for Priestly formation in the Syro-Malabar Church, Kakkanadu: Mount St. Thomas, 2007.
8. Daniel K.N., Udayamperoor Soonahadosinte Kanonakal, (Malayalam) Thiruvalla: St. Thomas Publications, 1952.

9. Elias Kuriakose Chavara, Chavarayachante Samboornna Krithikal: Nalagamangal (Vol. 1), Mannanam: CMI Central Publishing Committe, 1981.
10. Ferroli D., The Jesuits in Malabar (Vol. 1 & Vol. 2) Bangalore, Dharmaram Publications, 1939 & 1951.
11. Geddes Michael, The History of the Church of Malabar, London: OUP, 1992.
12. Gosh C.Suresh, History of Education in India, Jaipur: Rawat Publications, 2007.
13. Hambye. E.R.,History of Christianity In India (Vol III), Bangalore: CHAI, 1997.
14. Koodapuzha Xavier, Christianity in India, Kottayam: OIRSI, 1998.
15. Koodapuzha Xavier, Priestly Formation in the Syro-Malabar Church, Kottayam.
16. Kuriakose Thomas, Collection of Letters from Malabar to Rome, Pune, JDV 2004.
17. Kuzhumpil Joseph, A Short Outline of St.Joseph's Apostolic Seminary Puthenpally: Travancore, Alwaye: SH League, 1920.
18. Muller F.X., The Sacred Books of the East, Delhi: Atlantic Publications, 1964 (Vol)
19. Mundadan Mathias, History of Christianity in India: from the Beginning up to the Midddle of Sixteenth Century (Vol. I), Bangalore: CHAI, 1989.
20. Mundadan Mathias, Traditions of St. Thomas Christians, Bangalore: St. Paul Publications, 1970.
21. Padinjarekkoottu Issac, Letters from Malabar to Rome, Pune, ISPCK 1998)
22. Paika Jobin, Chavarayachan: Charithrakaran Vismaricha Deerkhadarshi (Mal), Kottayam: Deepika Publications, 2014.
23. Puthiakunnel Thomas, Keralathile Seminarikal, Ernakulam: Vincentian Publication, 1968
24. Puthiakunnel Thomas, Syro-Malabar Clergy and their General Obligations, Ernakulam: Vincentian Press, 1964.
25. Sanmiguel Victor, Puthenpally Central Apostolic Seminary- 1888-1933, Ernakulam: Ravi Printers, 1933.
26. Sanu M.K, Jeevitham Thanne Sanshesham: Visudha Chavarayude Jeevitham (Mal), Kottayam: Manorama Books, 2015.
27. Thoma Benard Kathanar, Mar Thoma Christhianikal (Mal), Pala...1916.
28. Thomman Kathanar Paremmackal, Varthamanapusthakam (Mal), Translated by Malieackal John, Kottayam: OIRSI, 2014.
29. Varicatt Cherian, The Suriani Church of India and Her Quest for Autochthonous Bishops (1877-1896), Kottayam: OIRSI, 1995.

30. Webster C.B. John, Historiography of Christianity in India, New Delhi: OUP, 2012.
31. Xavier Barreto Angela & Zupanov G. Ines, Catholic Orientalism, New Delhi: OUP, 2015.
32. Zacharia Scaria, Randu Praceenakruthikal, (Malayalam) Changanacherry: DC Books, 1976.

Articles

1. Joshuva. T.J, 'Orthodox Seminariyude Adhunika Kalaghattam' (Mal) in Thomas O. And Thomas John (ed), Pazhaya Seminary Charithravum Sakshyavum, Kottayam: Orthodox Seminary Publication, 2016, pp. 29-42.
2. Koodapuzha Xavier, 'Priestly Formation in the Syro-Malabar Church' in Thondiparambil Joseph (Ed), Feed My Sheep, Alwaye: SH League, 2007, pp. 27-34.

Notes

1. The word priest has got number of different meanings, the meaning and the responsibility attached to the term priest differs from religion to religion. Basically it is the term used to indicate the person who officiate the rituals and ceremonies of a particular religion who has sufficient training and knowledge in this regard. India has got a very glorious priestly tradition from the early centuries onwards. Here in this study the term priest strictly indicates the Christian priest who is taking care of the liturgical activities of the worshipping community.
2. Mathias Mundadan, History of Christianity in India: From the beginning up to the Middle of the Sixteenth Century (up to 1542) (Vol. 1), Bangalore: CHAI, 1989, p. 186.
3. The word liturgy comes from the Greek word Leitourgia which means Public acts. The term liturgy is used to indicate the worshipping activities of the faithful community in Christianity. The Christian community from the beginning onwards had its own ways of worshipping God and in course of time it got organized.
4. Thomas Christian community is the group of Christian community who owes the origin of their community to the apostle St.Thomas in the first century CE.
5. Seminary is an institution established for the training of priests in the Christian community which has its beginning in the western world after the Trent Council (An official meeting of the Bishops of the Catholic Church held in 1546-1563) and has spread into other parts of the world. In Kerala the beginning of such institutions can be traced from second half of the 16th Century.
6. Cf; Mathias Mundadan, History of Christianity in India (Vol. 1); From the beginning up to the Middle of the Sixteenth Century, Bangalore: CHAI, 1989, pp. 185-190. The same details are also

given in, L.W.Brown, The Indian Christians of St.Thomas, Cambridge: Cambridge University Press, 1956, pp. 175-183.

7. Thomas Puthiakunnel, Syro-Malabar Clergy and their General Obligations, Ernakulam: Vincentian Press, 1964, p. 23.
8. Raphel Thattil, Priestly Formation in the Syro-Malabar Church (Unpublished Doctoral Dissertation submitted in Pontifical oriental Institute Rome in 1988) p. 28.
9. Cf:Xavier Koodapuzha, Priestly Formation in the Syro-Malabar Church, Kottayam: OIRSI, 1987, p. 31.
10. Xavier Koodapuzha,Priestly Formation in the Syro-Malabar Church, Kottayam: OIRSI, 1987, p. 32.
11. Sebastian Kuzhumpil, A Short Outline of St.Joseph's Apostolic Seminary Puthenpally (Travancore), Puthenpally: SH League, 1920, pp. 13-19.
12. Propoganda Fide is a department of the Roman Curia which is mainly dealing with the propagation of faith. The formations of the priests are coming under this commission.
13. Joseph Nidiri, The Changing Church of Kerala, Kottayam: OIRSI, 1987, p. 65.
14. Sebastian Kuzhumpil, A Short Outline of St.Joseph's Apostolic Seminary Puthenpally (Travancore), Puthenpally: SH League, 1920, p. 17. Also refer Zacharias OCD, History Album of St. Joseph's Apostolic Central Seminary, Verapoly –Puthenpally-Alwaye, Kochi: Ravi Printers, 1933, p. 34., Also refer V.Sanmiguel OCD, Puthenpally Central Apostolic Seminary 1888-1933, Ernakulam: Ravi Printers, 1933, p. 45.
15. References about these can be seen in various placesSebastian Kuzhumpil, A Short Outline of St.Joseph's Apostolic Seminary Puthenpally (Travancore), Puthenpally: SH League, 1920, p. 25. Also refer Zacharias OCD, History Album of St.Joseph's Apostolic Central Seminary, Verapoly –Puthenpally-Alwaye, Kochi: Ravi Printers, 1933, p. 36., Also refer V.Sanmiguel OCD, Puthenpally Central Apostolic Seminary 1888-1933, Ernakulam: Ravi Printers, 1933, p. 58.
16. Sermons are the instructions or speeches made by the priests in the parish. It was a custom among the Syrian Catholics to make sermons on every assembly of the community and through the assemblies they were communicating the ideas which they want to communicate.
17. This is extracted from the Chronicle of St.Thomas Forane Church Mylacombu near Thodupuzha Ref No: Book No. 2, page No. 23/1904.
18. This chart is actually compiled by extracting the information from the book: Cf. Thomas Joy, Making in the Millennium, Pune: ISPCK, pp. 23-28.

19. Annie Thomas, The role of Syrian Christians in the education of Women in Kerala (An unpublished doctoral dissertation submitted to the faculty of History of SSUS Kalady) 2004, p. 56.

5

Ecofeminism: The Reflection of the Affinity between the Subjugation of Women and the Human Domination of Nature in the Society

— *Ancymol Joy*

Introduction

In the modern society, the importance of preserving nature and environment has a vital role. All over the world, the people are suffering as a result of pollution, environmental hazards and the consequences of the projects in the name of development and progress. The aim of Eco-feminism is to make people aware of the truth that the environmental issues are not a separated one from the issues related to the human beings and the welfare of the society. So it is better to consideration all of these issues collectively. Eco-feminism has the viewpoint that cooperation, mutual respect and love help the development of the whole society. Eco-feminism tries to eliminate all sorts of dominations and exploitations and enhance the relationship with each other. Eco-feminism tries to contribute the chance to change the social construction of the subjugation of women and the nature.

Eco-Feminism: Significance

Eco-feminism is the key factor in dealing the relationship between two major components of the society which are women and nature of the environment. Eco-feminism portrays the picture which focuses how treats the women and nature in the men dominated society. In order to subjugate the women and nature, the eco-feminism this depends upon the patriarchal society. There is a link between the oppression of the women and the exploitation of nature in the present society so eco-feminism cannot be separated from the problems of environment and oppression of women because the women contributes inevitably in order to improve the socio-economic condition of her family. This study discusses how the subjugation of women and environmental issues are related to each other. Eco-feminist theory points out that domination of women in the patriarchal society is linked to the destruction of the environment. The connections between women and nature are interrelated and also environmental issues directly affect the women welfare and development.

Ecological deconstruction is a direct threat to the life of women in the modern society. Eco-feminism tries to restore the value of nature and dignity of women in the modern society. It is understood that one of the major problems is degradation of the environment in the modern society. Consequently, dumping of the wastes, consumption of the products and the exploitation of the natural resources have led to a catastrophic situation in the present society. An eminent researcher Mrs. Suka Joshua in her essay, “Atwood’s Abysmal World and its Vanished Visionary Gleam (An Ecocritical Investigation of Margaret Atwood’s Futuristic Novels)” expresses that “Eco-concerned writers often gives disturbing description of nature and its decline, intended to impugn both our ignorance and our developmental greed”.

Eco-feminism is a branch of feminism which holds the experimental, cultural and historical connections between the domination of women and nature. Eco-feminism highlights the issues evolved in the domination of the nature and women. Eco-feminism is the movement for the sustainability of nature, the preservation of the environment and also for the freedom and identity of women. The movement, Eco-feminism, reflects the connection between the degradation of the nature and the oppression and the subjugation of women in the patriarchal society. Eco-feminism combines the elements of both green movement and feminism. Eco-feminism deals with the oppression of the women and the exploitation of the nature. In *Postcolonial Ecocriticism: Literature, Animals, Environment* Graham Huggan and Helen Tiffin explains,

If women have been associated with nature, and each denigrated with reference to the other, it may seem worthwhile to attack the hierarchy by reversing the terms, exalting nature, irrationality, emotion and the human or non-human body as against culture, reason and the mind.

The reproductive capacity of both women and nature brings both these elements together and men continue to exploit nature and women in order to satisfy their greed. Eco-feminism gives the picture of the consequences of water pollution, deforestation, animal rights, the rights of women and other issues related to women and environment. This movement explains the connection between the nature and women and their function in the society as life maker and supporters. In earlier days women are considered as the care takers of the children and supporters of the family members. However, women have the relationship with nature mainly because of these biological and functional similarities. Eco-feminists consider that nurturing role of women and nature are associated with each other.

Eco-feminism mainly stands to ameliorate the nature and women from exploitation in the patriarchal society. Moreover, eco-feminism inculcate how women and nature have been exploited in the patriarchal society. It is important that the male dominated society should go away from the situations that exploit and subjugate women. Sushila Singh in "Feminism: The *Movement and the Ideology" describes, "According to the feminist doctrine, the subjugation and* oppression of women is a central fact of history, a key to most of our social and Psychological disorders".

The term Eco-feminism was introduced by Francoise D' Eaubonne, the French writer, in her book, *Le feminism Ou la Mort*, in 1974 in which she equated the exploitation of the nature is paralleled with the domination of women by men. Eco-feminists share the opinion that the exploitation and the oppression of women in the patriarchal society are similar to the domination and subjugation of nature by the patriarchal society. The devaluation and degradation of women and nature are linked with each other. The devaluation of women and nature is increasing rapidly due the technological developments which. In many cases, development leads women's work to be considered as less valuable than compared to men.

Eco-feminism is a multi-elemental perspective in which the subordination of women and nature are questioned and discussed and it also praises the harmony between the life givers of society such as women and nature. Eco-feminism serves as a common place of two movements such as feminism and Eco-criticism both deal with the study of the oppression of the women and nature in the male dominated society. Eco-feminism asks the questions such as what are the connection between women and nature and what is the necessity to study the relationship between these two elements of the society.

Andrew Bennet and Nicholas Royle in their book *An Introduction to Literature, Criticism and Theory* write that "Ecofeminism attends in particular to the figurative language in which women and nature are presented and it responds to ways in which nature and feminine are often linked in a gesture that denigrates both". Eco-feminism tries to dismantle the patriarchal society in which women and nature are oppressed and subjugated. Eco-feminists attribute the significance to the connection between nature and women which reasons are behind in the development of the society.

According to Eco-feminism the patriarchal society has opinion that women and nature are considered as simple objects to be manipulated, exploited and controlled for their own welfare and development. Plethora of writers and activists try to express on the importance of eco-feminism. The eminent writers such as Adrienne Rich, Mary Oliver, Gary Synder, Sara Orne Jewette, Alice Walker and Margaret Atwood have created awareness on the eco-feminism and also need of an hour for protection of the nature exploitation.

Eco-feminism has been developed on the basis of the study on the relationship between women and nature. Eco-feminism tries to highlight the fact that the human centered society of the present age is the result of the dualism and hierarchy which leads to ignorance of the importance of the material world. Eco-feminism tries to develop an ethical and moral society in which both human and material beings are members.

The main focus of the Eco-feminism movement

- The oppression and ill treatment of both nature and women in the modern society
- Wiping away all forms of male domination and to make the earth more living one which now is in a dangerous situation
- As a result of the primary responsibilities such as household activities, bearing and nurturing children women fail to make a position in the male dominated society.

- Over population and over exploitation of the natural resources are the main reasons of the natural and environmental degradation.
- Large numbers of natural disasters are the consequences of the advancement of the science and technology which are the result of the masculine power.
- The domination of women and earth by the masculine world has significance in the society. The devaluation of women is basically rooted in the degradation of the earth.
- The subjugation of the environment starts from the influence of the patriarchal structure in which nature is the mere object to be used for the needs of the human beings.

Though women are more close to the nature, there is no doubt that they sufferer in the case of environmental degradation. Women have social responsibilities such as taking care of children, tending crops, cooking and other household activities. Without destroying the balance of environment they are gathering wood and water and use it only for their daily usage.

They do not over exploit the natural resources for their own greed or satisfaction. So any technologies and developments which stand for the devaluation of nature lead to the subjugation of women as well. The deforestation and pollution of the environment lead to the issues of women who are more closely related to nature. So the devaluation and the over exploitation of the nature go together and these elements have interconnection with each other.

The decision makers of the society, the male figures, restrict women from accumulation of land and wealth, independent form of labour and take their own steps in the society. They are considered as the least tools to bear the children and the passive objects to perform only the household activities. Iqbal Kaur in his essay "Protest against Sexual Colonialism: Margaret Atwood's *Surfacing* and Kamala Das' *My Story* argues that "In the Male universe, men would like women to remain oppressed and suppressed. The idea of women as a tree and independent existent is intolerable to them".

Conclusion

In the contemporary society, the nature and women are well-versed in socio-economic development due to the independent working environment. However, they treated second grade by the male by dominating with behavirour, attitude and traditional customs. In order to improve the climatic condition and women welfare and development, the men have to consider the women and nature is equal to them and their has enormous power with them so as in the educational institution and at working place and living places, parents have to inculcate to their children that the women are so equal to men whereas treat them as their equal part and also teach them how to save the natural resources particularly the water and trees for better life. In this context the eco-feminism discusses how to behave more elite with women and nature for creating a better future to the society.

Works Cited

- Bennett, Andrew and Nicholas Royle. *An Introduction to Literature, Criticism and Theory,* Routledge, 2015.
- Huggan, Graham and Helen Tiffin. *Postcolonial Ecocriticism: Literature, Animals, Environment.*
- Investigation of Margaret Atwood's Futuristic Novels)." *Canadian Literature: An Overview,* edited by K. Balachandran, Sarup and Sons, 2007, p. 102.
- Kaur, Iqbal. "Protest against Sexual Colonialism: Margaret Atwood's *Surfacing* and Kamala Das' *My Story.*" *Gender and Literature,* D. K. Publishers, 1992, p.195.
- Routedge, 2010. Joshua, Suka. "Atwood's Abysmal World and its Vanished Visionary Gleam (An Ecocritical
- Singh, Sushila. "Feminism: The Movement and the Ideology." *Feminism: Theory, Criticism, Analysis,* Pencraft International, 2009.

6

Skill Development in Indian through Feminist Perspectives

— ***Dr. M.H. Hullur***

Abstract

In the emergency society, the conventional wisdom is the major national problem at the college and university level of education. On one hand, which provides equal opportunity for entry for all young people and then retaining in school those entering until they complete their degrees. This view is based on the belief that a college degree is the key to success in Indian society today. The major foundations funding higher education base their current policies on belief. This conventional wisdom is fine as far as it goes. However, of equal importance is the actual skill development and learning achieved by students while in higher education. The current perception is that our nation does fine on this objective.

With this perception, then entry has brought up the highest priorities for higher education. However, this conventional wisdom is considered to be limited. Further, recent evidence indicates that roughly one third of all students graduating in higher education today have made no progress in developing the critical skills needed for vocational success and for discharging the responsibilities of a citizen in a modern democracy. The study analyses how to eradicate and solve this problem and makes recommendations for this important issue.

Introduction

"Education, vocational training and lifelong learning are central pillars of employability, employment of workers and sustainable enterprise development" —International Labour Organisation

Skill development is critical for economic growth and social development. The demographic transition of India makes it imperative to ensure employment opportunities for more than 12 million youths entering working age annually. It is estimated that during the seven-year period of 2005-2012, only 2.7 million net additional jobs were created in the country. To enable employment ready workforce in the future, the youth need to be equipped with necessary skills and education. The country presently faces a dual challenge of severe paucity of highly-trained, quality labour, as well as non-employability of large sections of the educated workforce that possess little and no job skills.

The skill development issue in India is thus pertinent both at the demand and supply level. To meet the demand side challenge, consistent efforts are being made towards expansion of economic activities and creation of large employment opportunities. On the supply side, a simple look at the projected youth population provides a fair reason to believe that India has the strength to cater to this demand. However, the employability quotient is questionable and remains a major area of concern. Already huge gaps exist between the industry requirements and the level of skills of workers due to varied reasons including inadequate training infrastructures, inappropriate mix of skills and education, outdated curricula, limited industry interfaces and limited standards.

The skill development ecosystem in India is skewed towards a formal education system with limited vocational training. While the vocational training is in a dismal state both qualitatively and quantitatively, the higher education system itself is grappling with issues related to scale and quality. Moreover, there is disconnection between the formal education system and work requirements, compounding the challenges related to the skill gap. A concerted action is thus required on the supply side to ensure sustained employability of the Indian youth.

Extensive efforts to skill the workforce are required, both in quantity and quality. Transforming the skill development ecosystem and making it responsive to needs of both industry and citizens require a scalable, efficient and comprehensive vocational training ecosystem to meet future requirements. The policy brief looks into the bottlenecks associated with women's livelihoods and the importance of skill development interventions to tackle the same. Policy provisions for skill development of women have also been encapsulated.

Objectives of the Study

1. To study the need and importance of technical education to women.
2. To study the empowerment of women through skill development challenges and opportunities in India.
3. To suggest possible solutions to overcome the obstacles.

Data collection and Methodology

The descriptive method and secondary data have used in the study. The secondary data collected from various books, Research Article, Magazines, Research Journal, E-journal, Report of UGC, and Report of the higher education and Websites.

Current Female workforce Participation Rate [WPR] Scenario

Female workforce participation rate (WPR) in India stands at 31.8%, which is almost half of the male WPR at 73.2%. While north-eastern and hilly states have performed well on female WPR, with Mizoram having the highest WPR at 61.3%, the situation is worrisome in Haryana, Uttar Pradesh and Punjab, with WPR as low as 9% in the latter.

Table 1: Top 5 States State

Top 5 States State	*Female WPR*
Mizoram	***61.3%***
Himachal Pradesh	***59.4%***
Meghalaya	***58.9%***
Arunachal Pradesh	***56.1%***
Telengana	***52.1%***

Source: Labour Bureau 2013-14

Table 2: Bottom 5 States

State	*Female WPR*
Punjab	***9.4%***
Delhi	***10%***
Uttar Pradesh	***14%***
Jammu and Kashmir	***16.4%***
Haryana	***16.5%***

Source: Labour Bureau 2013-14.

According to a Mckinsey Global Institute study, India could boost its Gross Domestic Product [GDP] by $2.9 trillion by 2025, if female workforce participation rate is improved by 10 percentage points. This would be equivalent to bringing 68 million more women into the non-farm labour force. According National Sample Survey Organization (NSSO), there are over 30 lakh unemployed women in India in 2012. As on December, 2013, a total of 1.65 crore women had registered on employment exchanges. However, only 58.8 thousand women had been placed through these exchanges in the same year. Improving participation of women in the workforce would require improvements in access and quality of education, skill development and employment opportunities available to women.

The government of India has implemented various programs to enhance job opportunities in India- such as the Prime Minister's Employment Generation Program (PMEGP), National Livelihoods Mission, Deen Dayal Upadhayay Grameen Kaushalya Yojana (DDUGKY), Pradhan Mantri Kaushal Vikas Yojana (PMKVY) along with entrepreneurship development programs. With a pressing need to harness the demographic dividend that India enjoys, special focus has been skill development initiatives.

Skill Development and Women's Empowerment

Majority of the workforce in India is in the informal sector. Low income women workers in the informal sector due to the irregular nature of work and little bargaining power are amongst the most vulnerable groups in the Indian economy. The *National Policy for Skill Development and Entrepreneurship, 2015* envisions skill development as a vehicle for women's empowerment. To impart skills to women, the government has taken steps like the *Skill Development Initiative Schemes* under Directorate General of Employment and Training developing over 10,000 training providers under which 12.6 lakh woman have availed benefits. There are 402 women ITIs and 1134 women wings in ITIs, which provide training to 1,41,907 women annually. Furthermore, vocational training schemes for women are being run by 10 Regional Vocational Training Institutes (RVTIs). The government has proposed to open 8 more Regional Vocational Training Institutes. The major policy provisions for skill development with a special focus on women are discussed as follows.

National Policy on Skill Development and Entrepreneurship, 2015

The National Policy on Skill Development highlights that in order to improve the productivity of the economy, participation of women in the labour force have improved. The policy provides a roadmap for skill development, including the setting up of Ministry of Skill Development and convergence of skill development initiatives of other Ministries. It also outlines various interventions that the government must take up to catalyze skill development for women. The policy highlights the need to improve access to skill development for women. According to the policy,

Additional training and apprenticeship seats set up exclusively for women. While the skill development infrastructure in India is vast, it creates facilities dedicated to women. This also includes increasing the pool of women trainers. As per the policy, mechanisms

To provide certification to women trainers' new institutes for training of women trainers promoted. The policy mentions the need for gender mainstreaming of training. Women participation in vocational education and training is low as compared to men.

Need for special delivery mechanisms such as mobile training units, flexible afternoon batches along with on local needs based training.

Incorporation of women related issues in the guidelines for skill training procedures, such as issues of safe and gender sensitive training environment, employment of women trainers, equity in remuneration, and complaint redressal mechanism.

While Digital India is gaining momentum, there is need to incorporate ICT for providing skill development solutions as well. The policy announces the ***promotion of an internet or mobile based platform for women*** **employment.** The platform connects skilled women and employers. It focuses on women willing to re-enter the workforce after a break and those affected by migration. The government of India is implementing several schemes on skill development. Given below are some of the schemes which have a special focus on women's skill development.

Deen Dayal Upadhyay Kaushalya Vikas Yojana (DDU-KVY)

DDU-GKY, the erstwhile Aajeevika Skills, is the skill training and placement program of the Ministry of Rural Development (MoRD) carried out as part of the National

Rural Livelihoods Mission (NRLM). The DDU-GKY focuses on providing high quality skill training opportunities through Project Implementing Agencies (PIAs) to rural poor youth, though there is a special focus on women as mentioned below. It has an outcome-based design and the PIAs are required to place a minimum of 75 percent of those who are trained in jobs providing regular monthly wages. Also, there are special programmes for skill development under DDU-GKYH running in Jammu and Kashmir (Himayat), Left Wing Extremism Affected Districts (Roshni) and 10 percent of the programme funds are dedicated to the North-Eastern states.

The programme provides funding support for placement linked skilling projects ranging from INR 25,696 per person to over INR 1 lakh. Andhra Pradesh and Tamil Nadu have been recognized as Resource States under the scheme as they have successfully implemented skilling programmes.

The scheme has ***special focus on women*** and outlines provision to improve quality of impact amongst women beneficiaries **Improving Coverage-** The scheme ***mandates that 1/3rd of the seats would be covered by women***. Gram Panchayats have to undertake special efforts to improve participation of women under the programme by conducting special counseling sessions. To enhance coverage, the upper age limit for women has been revised up to 45, as against 35 years.

Support to Training and Employment Programme for Women (STEP)

The Key Sectors under to STEP are: Agriculture, Horticulture, Food Processing, Handlooms, Tailoring and Stitching, Handicrafts, Computer and IT, Gems and Jewellery, Travel and Tourism and Hospitality

The STEP program is a Central Sector Scheme of Ministry of Women and Child Development under which training is provided to poor and marginalized women in traditional trades to improve employability. The scheme is intended to benefit women who are in the age group 16 and above. Under the programme, grants-in-aid are provided by the central government to societies, voluntary organizations, and cooperatives providing skills in sectors ranging from agriculture to hospitality. Training courses under STEP would primarily be of 3 months or 6 months duration, with total assistance per beneficiary at Rs 18000 and Rs 28000 respectively. The maximum number of beneficiaries per project will not exceed 200. As of February, 2015, a total funding of Rs 400.21 lakhs was released under the scheme. Amongst the states, Manipur received the maximum funding under the scheme, followed by Madhya Pradesh and Assam. A total of ***24,037*** women beneficiaries have been impacted under the scheme. With limited participation in the workforce, the potential of women remains untapped. Effective implementation of the envisioned skill development interventions is needed to make them key stakeholders in development.

Skill Development Challenges in India

Alongside the daunting challenge of skilling millions of youth entering workforce each month, India also faces a huge challenge of evolving a skill development system that can equip the workforce adequately to meet the requirements of the industry. The workforce needs to be trained across four levels, from the high end specialised skills for 'White Collar' jobs to the low-level skills of the 'Rust Collar' jobs. Moreover, these skills have adequately linked to the available job opportunities.

Several factors have inhibited the skill development eco-system in India to scale up to the desired levels. The skill development system in India is plagued with multiple issues related to awareness, perception, cost, quality and scale.

Inadequate scale, limited capacity: The existing infrastructure, both physical and human, is grossly inadequate considering the projected demand for skilled labour. While there is a need to create additional capacity in existing institutes, at the same time there is a need to create an adequate infrastructure even in small towns and villages. In terms of faculty, too, the training infrastructure is inadequate. The corresponding to the current seating capacity of about 1.7 million trainees at ITIs, there is a need of almost 85,000 trainers. As against this, the seating capacity for various trainers' programme of DGET is just 4,438, which is far from adequate to meet the requirement.

Awareness, mindset and perception issues: Skill development in India is way below the requirements due to a lack of awareness on the type of courses as well as information on the ensuing career prospects. More importantly, there is limited acceptance of skill development courses as a viable alternative to formal education. Skilling is often viewed as the last resort meant for those who have not been able to progress in the formal academic system. This is partly to do with the lack of integration between the two options and also due to rising aspirations for white collar jobs which necessitate higher qualifications. Moreover, skill development is often associated with blue collar jobs, which is largely perceived to be of low dignity and provides low wages and salaries. The perceived 'stigma' associated with skill development has resulted in low enrolments in vocational education courses. The aspiration mismatch that exists in India can be gauged from the example of the construction sector, which has a huge requirement of workforce with low level skills. The construction sector in Punjab faces a shortage of workers locally, and depends on the migrant workforce from Uttar Pradesh, Bihar and Jharkhand.

Cost concerns: Skill development initiatives in India continue, largely dependent upon the government funds or public-private ventures. Owing to high capital requirements and low return on investments, skill development is often looked at as a non-scalable model and remains underinvested. Additionally, a fee-based model also faces challenges as prospective students are often unwilling or unable to pay high fees for training. Even the bank's willingness to lend for skill development activities is low as educational loans are perceived as high risk products due to uncertainty with respect to future employment.

Quality concerns: There is a serious mismatch between the industry's requirements and the skills imparted in educational and training institutes, especially for the mid-level skills requiring some expertise on handling of machinery. To tackle this problem, considerable improvement of the quality of training is needed. The issue relates to the quality of infrastructure, trainers, as well as curricula and pedagogy. In terms of infrastructure, the institutes often lack appropriate machinery to give students hands-on training. Even the course curricula often are outdated, redundant and non-standardised. Additionally, the lack of industry-faculty interaction on course curricula leads to irrelevant training modules. The availability of good quality trainers is also a key concern.

The quality of trainers is affected due to limited efforts towards re-training and skill improvement of trainers. There is a lack of focus on development of trainers with a clear career path which can make this an aspiration career choice and can ensure regular adequate supply of good-quality trainers in every sector. While there is a need to constantly upgrade the training infrastructure and pedagogy, it is very expensive. This restricts the pace of modernisation and upgradation. Likewise, the process of standardisation is challenging in India. A significant portion of total employment falls under the unorganised segment, where it is extremely difficult to sensitise the employers on the importance of occupational standards, job roles and qualification packs.

Mobility concerns

In India, educational qualification is generally preferred over vocational training as former is associated with better employment opportunities, in terms of pay as well as quality of work. Additionally, there is limited mobility between formal education and vocational training in India due to lack of equivalent recognition for the latter; a student enrolled in vocational training often cannot migrate to institutes of higher education due to eligibility restrictions. However, under the on-going National Skills Qualification Framework (NSQF), attempts are being made to address the mobility issue by recognition of prior learning and establishing a credit system for skills, knowledge and experience gained by an individual either formally or informally. NSQF is expected to enable multiple-entry and exit between vocational education, skills training, general education, technical education and job markets.

Key Issues and Challenges in Skill Development

As noted earlier, the aim of skill development, particularly in case of women which is prepared them for jobs and improved the performance of women workers by enhancing the quality of work in which they are engaged.

The NSDC has identified a few of the *major challenges, which need to be addressed for building a conducive ecosystem, of skill development for the women workforce.* These are as follows,

- The large number of women who need to be trained since currently only 2% of the female workforce is formally trained
- Inadequacies in the quality and relevance of TVET (Technical and vocational employment training in India)
- Inadequate Infrastructure, acute shortage of trained women workers, poor quality of training

- Lack of mechanisms to judge and certify quality
- Inequity in access to TVET for women
- Low level of education of potential women trainees that limits training of women in the formal sector
- Lack of recognition of prior learning of potential women trainees
- Relatively high opportunity cost of learning involved for training women.

The major challenges noted are few in number but represent a complexity of issues involved Additionally, it is argued that the empowerment practice has to go beyond its focus on women to gender. A focus on gender would imply an emphasis on strategic needs such as leadership and advocacy, rather than a simple focus on basic needs. The concept of gender will also, encourage an understanding and an analysis of power relations, and enforces the idea of developing capabilities rather than simply skills.

Another important point that cannot be left out is the potential advantage of "demographic dividend" that India has over many other countries. "The demographic dividend arises as an asset for India due to expected decline in dependency ratio in the country. The dependency ratio (ratio of dependent to working age population) of India has declined from 0.8 in 1991 to 0.73 in 2001, and is expected to further decline to 0.59 by 2011. Low dependency ratio gives India a cost advantage and helps in improving India's competitiveness." This demographic dividend is expected to last until around 2035.16.

Hence, India has to act now and get the training and skill development right to benefit from this demographic dividend, to create a global pool of skilled persons. However, if the demographic dividend is not turned into an opportunity now, and if India fails to deliver, this demographic dividend in about 25 years may actually become a handicap. Besides the demographic dividend, another factor that adds to the urgency for improved skill development is the increasing number of newly educated youth, especially women, who would like to seek employment in the service sector. The education and skill development sector has not adequately responded to this emerging need, making it imperative to provide skill development and training in marketable skills and services.

It is therefore clear, that there is a dire and urgent need for a paradigm shift in the skill development sector, in favour of innovations, improvements and high quality training. It is also observed, that the concept of training and skill development needs to move beyond the conventional goal of imparting technical and managerial competencies, to playing a broader role of even including basic literacy, numeracy, critical social and political awareness, awareness about gender, and enhancing life skills. Such interventions by their nature encourage self esteem among women and overall personality development. It is also urged that for skill development to be more effective, training needs to bend towards developing the kind of skills learnt. In other words, the need is to enhance or adapt traditional skills to general principles should be taken into consideration in developing training programmes, including

1. ***Relevance to the labour market:*** requires communication with markets about their needs. The public and private employers should take part in developing the curricula and invest in it. A local market study is useful for learning about current and future employment needs. Training should be demand-driven.
2. ***Gender capacity building:*** teachers and employers participating in training programmes should receive gender training so they avoid stereotyping and aware of social constructions and norms. As part of developing competencies,

there should be an analysis of the relative participation of young men and young women and equality of resources provided. One objective promotes each gender's participation in non-stereotypical areas.

3. ***Development of competencies:*** analysis of the necessary competencies and sub-competencies should be made nationally and locally. This ensures they reflect the standardization necessary to make them nationally acceptable while also taking local context into account. The employers who validate the skills developed by trainees should participate in certifying the competencies.
4. ***Development of 'soft skills':*** employers need workers with attributes such as timeliness, productivity, networking ability and teamwork. In many countries, it takes time to inculcate these qualities. Customs should be respected, but trainees need to learn the qualities that industries require. This also helps employers to adapt their practices and expectations to the local context.
5. ***Long-term funding:*** funding from international donors is often short term, so other sources of funding must be found. But empowering young women and addressing long-standing gender discrimination requires long-term commitments. Ongoing government support is needed, and international funding agencies also should consider longer-term commitments to protect initial costly investments in infrastructure, materials and teacher training. But requiring trainees to pay counterproductive for females, because families who have to pay are more likely to pay for males. One possibility is a system of grants for girls' participation, which would help to motivate families.

6. ***Access for trainees:*** easy and affordable access and availability of transportation to the site are important, especially where the training centre is located at a distance. Mobile training centres can also be considered. Another way to reach trainees is to integrate vocational training into the formal school system. Plans for such an approach must consider the timing of the training to address security concerns that could affect the participation of young women and girls.

Discussions and analyses

The Indian Government has laid a special focus on expanding and improving the skill education and training in the country. The New Policy on Skill Development and Entrepreneurship contains several initiatives which, if implemented earnestly it goes a long way in minimizing the demand-supply gap and challenges related to skill mismatch with industry requirements. With increased thrust on manufacturing under the 'Make in India' programme, the need for revisiting and improving India's skill development mechanism becomes all the more critical. It has been globally recognised that an efficient vocational education and training plays a critical role in the industrial development and manufacturing success, as in the case of economies like Germany and China. The study of skill development models of three countries done in this report highlights some best practices that can be utilised in India's skill development eco-system. Integration of skill development with formal education system, mobilisation of students for skill development by removing misapprehensions and perceptions about vocational trades, investing in creation of new training capacities for students as well as teachers, utilisation of idle public infrastructure to provide skill training in remote corners of the country, encouraging industry to actively participate in training through provision of apprenticeship as well as through direct involvement in curriculum design and teachers training, adopting innovative skill development delivery mechanisms are the much-needed steps to meet the skill related challenges today. There is a scope of international collaboration and assistance in India's skill development initiatives at almost all levels, including for creating awareness and capacities, setting standards, improving quality, as well as providing placement opportunities.

Recommendation and Suggestion: based on the study valued suggestion given below, they are:

- Skill development programmes to be run by one ministry
- Gender sensitive policy
- Expansion of training institutes and provision of basic infrastructure
- Up gradation of the craftsmen training scheme
- Provision of vocational training in schools
- Identifying and making efforts to change basic and nuanced socio-cultural values
- Making the private sector responsible for skill development in the country
- Accessible and affordable training
- Support services beyond training
- High quality training that matches the changing needs of the market
- **Setting up of migration support centres (MSC)** MSCs would be set up to look after the needs of the vulnerable population, especially women. They set up both inside the state, as well as outside the state in areas where a large number of DDUKVY trainees have been placed. Funding for this is provided to the State Rural Livelihoods Mission (SRLM) which may take it up on its own or with the support of the PIA.
- **Training of trainers**: the scheme has special focus on establishing training centres with focus

on women trainers. This is in line with the National Policy of Skill Development, which aims to increase the number of women trainers. Furthermore, women trainers are being trained; the scheme mandates at least one women manager.

- **Post placement support**: the responsibility of the PIAs to conduct post placement counselling sessions for the candidates, and especially for the women, to help them in adapting to new environment.

Conclusion

The emerging global economy demands more high-skilled and better-educated quality workers than earlier years. While there is tremendous need to expand vocational education system, including through open schooling to meet the learning needs and skill development challenges, particularly of women, it is highly essential to maintain quality and ensure that the training is responsive to market demands. There is also the necessity of collaboration with industries to make the curriculum market and employment oriented so that learners get adequate employment. Each component of the vocational programme needs to be seriously reviewed given that large percentage of potential employees requires quality training to match the global competitiveness. National Institute of Open Schooling [NIOS] has the unique provision of offering academic along with vocational courses. This makes education holistic with the integration of academic with vocational courses and thus, learners are provided education for life as well as livelihood. However, there is a need to make the courses linking to job opportunities and market realities and ensure that the learners get decent employment.

References

- Abrahart, A et al (2009), "Reforms in The Indian Vocational Education and Training System", In Vocal, Vol. 7, 2008-09, pp. 107-116.

- Bennell, P (1999), "Learning to Change: Skills Development among the Economically Vulnerable and Socially.
- Central Universities". ugc.ac.in
- Choudaha, Rahul (2014-05-09). "Three Solutions for Reforming Indian Higher Education Dr Education: Global Higher Education Research". Www.dreducation.com
- Excluded in Developing Countries", Employment and Training Papers, 43, Employment and Training Department, International Labour Office, Geneva
- Higher Education, National Informatics Centre, Government of India". Education.nic.in. Archived from the original on 18 July 2011.
- India Country Summary of Higher Education" (PDF). World Bank.
- International Center for Research on Women, Washington, D.C., 2009.
- International Centre for Research on Women, 'Can Economic Empowerment Reduce Vulnerability of Girls and Young
- International Labour Organization, 'Employment for Social Justice and a Fair Globalization: Overview of ILO programmes,' ILO, Geneva, June 2010.
- International Labour Organization, 'Employment, Incomes and Equality: A strategy for increasing productive employment in Kenya', ILO, Geneva, 1972.
- International Labour Organization, 'Equality at Work: Tackling the challenges', Report of the Director-General, Global report under the follow-up to the ILO declaration on fundamental pinciples and rights at work, International Labour Conference, 96th Session, 2007.
- Journal of Knowledge Management, Vol. 13 Iss: 5 pp. 345 - 358.
- Latest Statistics on Indian Higher Education". DrEducation.com. 2012-07-17.
- Matt Lynley (9 July 2012). "The World's Best Engineering Schools". Business Insider.
- MHRD, Annual Report on Higher Education in India- 2015-2016.
- MHRD.gov.in.
- National Network of Education (2008-10-06). "'Mobile Study Centres have increased student participation' – IGNOU VC, Universities News – By". Indiaedunews.net. Retrieved 2011-05-03. List of State Universities" (PDF). 27 May 2011.
- Private Universities – University Grants Commission". ugc.ac.in. 1 August 2011. Archived from the original on 1 August 2011. Retrieved 1 August 2011.
- Ranjan Ravi, Naveen (2015). "Structure and Organisation of Higher Education in India : A Macro-Perspective" (PDF). Indian Journal of Educational Studies: An Interdisciplinary Journal. 2.

- Reforming higher education with transparency – University World News". Www.universityworldnews.com. Statistics – Ministry of Human Resource Development" (PDF). mhrd.gov.in.
- Rukmini S. (2015-08-04). "Only 8.15% of Indians are graduates, Census data show". The indu.
- Surinder Batra, (2009),"Strengthening human capital for knowledge economy needs: an Indian perspective",
- Women to HIV? Emerging insights', ICRW, Washington, D.C., 2010.

7

A Study on Elected Representatives of Dalit Women and Human Rights Prespective

— ***Dr. T.S. Bala Gomala,***
Dr. S. Baluchamy

Abstract

Dalit women are often trapped in highly patriarchal societies. The severe discrimination they face from being both a Dalit and a woman, makes them a key target of violence and systematically denies them choices and freedoms in all spheres of life. This endemic intersection of gender-and-caste discrimination is the outcome of severely imbalanced social, economic and political power equations. Dalit women suffer from severe limitations in access to justice and there is widespread impunity in cases where the perpetrator is a member of a dominant caste, above the Dalits in the caste system. Dalit women are therefore considered easy targets for sexual violence and other crimes, because the perpetrators almost always get away with it. For example, in India, studies show that the conviction rate for rapes against Dalit women is under 2% compared to a conviction rate of 25% in rape cases against all women in India. Caste and gender discrimination in the delivery of education health care, water, sanitation and other basic services are also major obstacles for Dalit women severely impacting on their welfare and opportunities. This discrimination has been documented repeatedly by UN agencies and major international human rights and development NGOS. Dalit women often work in modern slavery and are key targets for trafficking. They are often used as debt slaves in brick kilns, garment industries and agriculture. 98% of those forced into the dehumanising work of manual scavenging, removing human waste by hand, are also Dalit women. Dalit women are uniting against one of the world's most gruesome and effective systems of oppression the intersection of caste and gender discrimination of Dalit women and movements across of the world are growing stronger and are connecting to each other and reaching out to decision-makers and people of the world.

Introduction

Women experience endemic gender-and-caste discrimination and violence as the outcome of severely imbalanced social, economic and political power equations. Their socio-economic vulnerability and lack of political voice, when combined with the dominant risk factors of being Dalit and female, increase their exposure to potentially violent situations while simultaneously reducing their ability to escape. Dalit women Caste, class and gender discrimination prevents Dalit women from enjoying their basic human rights, particularly to dignity, equality and development. Atrocities and violence against Dalit women are both a means of sustaining systemic discrimination, as well as a reaction when particularly untouchability practices and caste norms are challenged or not adhered to. Impunity for this discrimination and violence is then used as a means to preserve the existing caste and gender disparities. Before Dalit women can enjoy their human rights, and before the Millennium Development Goals can be achieved, discrimination, violence and impunity must stop.

Social exclusion as a concept is more suitable and comprehensive term to explain the precarious conditions in which Dalits are living in India and social and cultural exclusion is natural outcome of the caste system. Dalits, poverty stricken, landless agricultural labourers, economically impoverished, socially and educationally backward, politically unorganized and culturally dubbed as savage people, are highly vulnerable for social discrimination in India. Majority of them are landless agricultural labourers.

They served as cheap labourers in unorganized sector. They are economically dependent on the other people, mostly landed gentry in villages. Politically highly unorganized as their number is less comparative to the other dominant castes. Their minority status is the main cause of 'powerlessness'. Majority of them come under the category of below poverty line familes. They are known as underprivileged classes and socially and culturally excluded collectivities in India. Dalits, have faced considerable discrimination in the past and still do so in several spheres of social life. While the state have embarked on economic development. The Constitution of India ensured Equality, Freedom, and Fraternity. All discriminations based on caste, class, ethnicity and other forms of discriminations have been considered illegal and punishable under the law. All are equal before the law. The universal adult franchise, introduction of reservation of seats in the Parliament, State Legislatures and other constitutional bodies for the Dalits have ushered in an egalitarian society.

Statement of the Problem

The establishment of a democratic society coupled with planned social changes and social reconstruction programmes further helped in giving impetus in transforming Indian society from conservative to more egalitarian in nature. The effects of changes are being felt in every aspect of social system, it may be rapid in some cases and it may also be slow in others. These changes have had their impact on the women, more so on Dalit women, as they are backward among the backwards. The process of social change among them is slow in comparison to the women of upper strata in the Indian society. Dalit women were thus least affected by the process of social change and their social, economic and political position was far from satisfactory. A study on the changing status of Dalit women in India is thus sociologically necessary and meaningful not only to understand the broad patterns and processes of socialchanges, but it is also quite essential to understand the emerging patterns of leadership among the most oppressed bottom collectivities of hierarchical social system. Such an attempt will also reveal the overall structural changes in the Indian society. the socio-economic, educational, political and cultural background how Dalit woman have been able to perform altogether a new and different roles as member of PRI at grass root level is a issue raised for an empirical exploration.

Objectives of the study

- To explore into the socio-economic and educational status of Dalit women.
- To assess the political awareness among Dalit women.
- To examine their political aspirations of Dalit women
- To understand the process of socialchange among Dalit women in the rural society.

Methodology of the study

This study was undertaken with the primary objective of studying political participation of elected women representatives belonging to Dalit community in PRI's and rural Dalit women are now turned in traditional values, beliefs and culture that is marked by male predominance, which tend to marginalize them. The elected women representatives are not effectively participating in the decision making process at grassroots level governance i.e., PRI's due to patriarchy, gender biases, illiteracy, dependency, poverty and so on. It is a matter of serious concern and representation that empowerment of Dalit women is encountered by the male dominance and proxy representation. The study also concentrated to examine the social, economic and demographic profiles which are playing a vital role to influence level of participation of

Dalit elected women representatives; and relatively more number of indicators of participation was included for this study with a view to determine the effectiveness of women's participation in PRI's.

Methods of Data Collection

Information regarding the profile of the Dalit women elected representatives and nature of their self-perceived participation in decision making was gathered through structured interviews. Since the study is based on survey design, interview method is considered as the most appropriate method of data collection.

Initiatives of the Government for Improvement of the Condition of Dalit Women

The participation of Dalit women representatives by seeking their opinion on the reservation for women, female education and socio- economic participation of political career and their participation in decision making and Finally the respondents role in decision making in Grama Panchayats and women's attendance in meeting's, average time spent in village matters, nature of issues handled, ways of improvise their participation and advantages of their participation; and Influence of family on the political career of Dalit women elected women representatives and future of political career. Dalit women victim-survivors of violence is too often effectively stymied by different actors the perpetrators, their caste community, police, the traditional village panchayats or formal elected panchayats.

With the objective to facilitate a faster socio-economic development of the Scheduled Caste/Scheduled Tribe and support them with various welfare measures particularly on education, to end their social exclusion and economic deprivation and speed up the process of integrating them with the national main stream, the Government of Tamil Nadu implements of several welfare programmes. All the departments of the Government to specific allocations for the benefit of Scheduled Caste/Scheduled Tribe from their plan programmes as special component plan. In addition special central assistance is funded by the Government of India for various welfare schemes. Scheduled Caste families do not own house sites of their own, the Government of Tamil Nadu provides them a house site not exceeding 3 cents in rural areas and 1½ cents in urban area free of cost by acquiring lands owned by private persons. These sites are assigned in the name of the elder women member of the family. Apart from this, houses are also being constructed free of cost in the above sites under the group house scheme.

The Development and empowerment of Dalit women is one of the most crucial issues of today. It is universally accepted that there have not considerable governmental efforts, on one of the sections of women namely Scheduled Caste and Scheduled Tribe women lag woefully behind others in development and they continue to be among the weakest and the exploited. Moreover, women in transition economics are finding that their specific skills are becoming absolute. In weaker sectionswomen play a major role, especially in economic field. Inspite of the development taking place all around, it has to be conceded that the bulk of the Scheduled Caste Women will continue to live and earn livelihood in their own environment.

Recommendations

Women and girls affected by caste-based discrimination are particularly vulnerable to various forms of sexual violence, forced and ritual prostitution, trafficking, domestic violence and punitive violence when they seek justice for crimes committed. Measures should be taken to increase protection from these crimes and to tackle impunity and discrimination in access to justice. Such measures can include police and judicial training and monitoring, legal assistance for prosecution of crimes, strengthening laws against domestic violence and other forms of violence against women, awareness campaigns to help prevent exploitation, and investing resources into education for women and girls affected by caste-based discrimination and State parties of caste-affected countries should initiate a process of dialogue with civil society organisations in framing policies, laws and programmes to eliminate multiple forms of violence and discrimination against Dalit women. Legal and structural mechanisms can only function effectively if the attitude and perception of people are changed. Law enforcement agencies, the judiciary, civil society and other stakeholders must combine efforts to enable such change and firm measures must be taken by state agencies to punish officials who neglect or violate legal and other statutory provisions.

Conclusion

The Government should frame more effective laws, implement and protect human rights of women. Protect all the human rights of women organization and women forum to protect women rights and proper functioning of human rights organizations and Human rights 'cell' is required to be made to see and register the cases of violations of human rights and educate to all the people about the human rights issue of development and the implementation of the Universal declaration must be approached realistically Court trials should be time bound to secure speedy justice for victims of violence and atrocities. This would be similar to time bound investigation and charge sheets for the police. National Human Rights Institutions in every caste-affected country are encouraged to bring out an annual white Paper to appraise their performance in relation to caste and gender-based human rights violations. Promote SHG with finance for promoting the human rights of women. Enforcement of existing laws against violations by Government, role of NGOs, educating women on their rights, encouraging women in reporting violations to the concerned higher authority are suggested by respondents for the elimination of violations of human rights of women.

References

- Ahuja and Mukesh (1996) Widows; Role Adjustment and Violence, Wishwa Prakashan Delhi.
- Ajitavasth and Shubhmohan Singh (2015), Human Rights and Psychiatry in South Asia, Mental Health in South Asia: Ethics, Resources, Programs and Legislation, International Library of Ethics, Law, and the New Medicine Volume 58, 2015.
- Anand. V.K . (2001) Human Rights pioneer Books, Delhi – 110009. Bhar Gava G.S. (2001) Human Rights of Dalit Societal Violation, Gyan publishing House, 5, Ansari Road, New Delhi – 110002
- Bhattacharya (2004) Behind Closed Doors: Domestic Violence in India, sage Publications, New Delhi.
- Bishakha Data (2004) A Study of All Women Panchayats in Maharashtra.
- Dorothy Thomas (2003) Woman's Human Rights; from visibility to accountability, Bangolore.
- Durga Das Basu (1994) Human Rights in Constitutional Law, prentice hall of India private Ltd, New Delhi
- Dutta R.K .(2003) Women Empowerment Reference Press, New Delhi.
- Marjorie Agosin (2003) Woman Gender and Human Rights: A Global perspective, Rawat publication, Jaipur, NewDelhi-110002.
- Mehtaneenavarma (1999) Human Rights under the Indian constitution. The philosophy and judicial Gerrymandering, Deep & Deep publications Pvt, Ltd, NewDelhi-110027.
- Mendelsohn (1998) Violence against Dalits, New Delhi-110002.

8

Tribal Women Empowerment – An Example From Minicoy, Lakshadweep

— ***Joel Oommen Muzhangody***

Abstract

Scheduled Tribes of India especially their Women members are generally associated with the atrocities affecting their Women empowerment. Often they are educationally backward and their capabilities deprived. In this largely dominant image the scheduled tribe women of Lakshadweep especially that of Minicoy stands out among the rest. Their unique history, social background, local governance, economic scenario etc have devised a template such that their Women play equal role in all fields and sometimes dominant role than their male counterparts. This paper is an attempt to analyze the reasons of empowerment and the challenges faced by the tribal women of Minicoy.

Key Words: Empowerment, Lakshadweep, Minicoy, Scheduled Tribe, Women.

Introduction

The scheduled tribe (ST) population is 104.2 million, which is 8.6 percent of the total population of India (Census 2011). Madhya Pradesh, Maharashtra, Orissa, Gujarat, Rajasthan, Jharkhand, Chhattisgarh, Andhra Pradesh, West Bengal, and Karnataka are the states having a large number of ST populations. The overall areas inhabited by the tribal population constitute a significant part of the underdeveloped areas of the country. About 93 per cent of them live in rural areas and are engaged in agriculture and allied activities. The socio-demographic figures clearly reveal the disadvantaged position of the STs compared to other category of population. The literacy rate among the STs in India is 63.1 per cent (NSSO, 2010), which is lower than the national literacy rate i.e. 72.8 per cent (Census, 2011). The dropout rate among the STs is 70.5 which are much higher than the dropout rate of all categories i.e. 49.15 percent. The sex ratio among the STs is 990 which is relatively better than the general population i.e. 940 (Census, 2011). The infant mortality rate among the ST children is 62.1 which is 57 for the other social groups. The child mortality rate among the tribes is 35.8 which is much higher than the other social groups i.e. 18.4 percent. The work force participation rate (WFPR) is 60 among the ST population and that is higher than the total population i.e. 53percent (NSSO, 2010). The WFPR indicates that majority of the ST population are engaged in unorganized sector without any job security. This paper attempts to study Scheduled Tribes of Lakshadweep with emphasis on Minicoy Island in this background. Their social indicators are in sharp contrast to their peers in rest of India. The paper tries to understand the causes behind this phenomenon.

Significance of the Study

The demographic figures reveal that the tribal population is the most disadvantaged, exploited and the neglected lot in India. Despite certain constitutional provisions, they are backward compared to the general population, even their situation is worse than the Schedule Caste (SC) and Other Backward Class (OBC) population (Xaxa, 2012). Majority of the tribes used to reside in the remote forest areas, remain isolated, untouched by civilization and unaffected by the development processes. This situation has changed to a great extent over the years. As long as the tribes have access to resources generated from the forest, they have no difficulties in satisfying their basic needs. In turn they have an interest in preserving the forest as it is their life support system. But large scale industrialization, urbanization and exploitation of natural resources due to deforestation to meet the urban and industrial demands has greatly affected the livelihood pattern. This trend has been responsible for displacing large number of tribes from their habitations (Nathan & Xaxa, 2012; Singh, 2012).

More than after Seventy Years of Independence, the picture of Scheduled Tribes of India hasn't been glossy worse for tribal women. It is in this regard at the Southern most corner of our frontier lies a small territory which provides lessons in Women Empowerment worth emulating. This paper attempts to analyse the social structure of Minicoy in this regard.

Methodology

The study uses both primary and secondary data. The primary data was collected by direct interaction and interview with natives of Minicoy. Field level interview was administered. Various secondary data was collected from Central Government reports and periodicals. The study was exploratory in nature.

Tribal Women of Lakshadweep

94.5% (2011) of the people of Lakshadweep falls under Scheduled Tribe category .The excellent craftsmanship of the STs in Lakshadweep has made them popular across the globe. Some of them own land in these islands while others work as labourers. The majority of the STs in Lakshadweep follow Islam as religion. Lakshadweep ranks at 5th position (per 1000 persons among 5 years and above) among STs (NSSO, 2010). The ST literacy rate in island region is comparatively higher compared to other regions, despite that the gross enrolment ratio among scheduled tribe (ST) students in class I-VIII is quite low in the island region.

Lakshadweep has a literacy rate of 80.18% for tribal women only bettered by Mizoram (86.05%) compared to 58.11% literacy rate of tribal women from Kerala. Overall literacy rate of Lakshadweep (81.56) is way higher compared to other tribal pockets in India. Undoubtedly this has uplifted the tribal women of Lakshadweep than their peers in rest of India.

Lakshadweep

Out of a total of 36, only 10 islands of Lakshadweep are inhabited by the local populace – Andrott, Amini, Agatti, Bitra, Chetlat, Kadmath, Kalpeni, Kiltan, Minicoy and Kavaratti; the latter being the headquarters of the Union Territory. The 11th island, Bangaram, holds a resort. Human communities of Lakshadweep are primarily *Koya, Malmi and Melacheri*, belonging in most cases to the Shafi School Muslims of the Sunni sect. The earlier inhabitants of Lakshadweep were Hindus who had migrated from the Malabar Coast of Kerala and were converted to Islam in the 7th century AD by Hazrat Ubaidulla, an Arab Saint. As per the Census 2011, the total population of Lakshadweep is 64,429 of which male and female are 33,106 and 31,323 respectively, spread over a 32 sq km of land area with a population density of 2013 per sq km.

Even though there is dominance of Islam, the social structure is based on the matrilineal kinship and caste system that reflects the Hindu customs of Kerala – a custom that in recent decades has significantly lost its grip, with a rise in nuclear families and male heads of households.

Koya: The community has been named from a term derived from khoia meaning 'respect' in the local dialect. The community was formerly known as the Tarawad referring to the principle families or the Karnavan who were heads of Tarawads. The Koyas are generally land owners and a class enjoying great respect in the society. This and the other classes speak Malayalam but a local dialect does exist – Vattezhuthu, which has Tamil and Canarese influences.

Malmi: The sailor community, named after 'muaellim,' a word of Arabic origin, meaning, 'one who shows the way'. Thus, Malmis are the sailor community that plied the indigenous boats 'odam' to serve the Koyas by transporting rice and other essential goods from the mainland. The traditional dress of Lakshadweep is fairly simple, with men wearing white or coloured lungis with its ends stitched together and women wearing kachi, the unstitched version, around their waists tied in place with silver belts. Women also cover their head with thattam – a kind of a long scarf, and wear a fitted long sleeved bodice with embroidered fronts. Ornaments are worn in profusion, with multiple ear and nose piercing fairly common. Today, however, the practice of purdah and the advent of salwar kameez is changing the traditional clothing of the women in the communities here. Men too have changed their attire from being generally bare chested to modern day shirts.

Melacheri: Originally they were the community of landless tree climbers, plucking coconuts from trees owned by Koyas and tapping sweet-toddy. Belonging to the class that provides labour, Melacheri faced a level of social obstracisation in terms of marriage into koya families and certain rituals in the past. The divide has slowly levelled out in the present context.

The Minicoy Island

Among the ten inhabited islands, Minicoy Island is the southernmost island of Lakshadweep. It is referred as Maliku Island by its natives. The island is located between 8 15' and 8 20' north latitudes and between 73 1 and 73 05' east longitudes. The total area of the island is about 4.4 km2 including the attached islet of Viringli, known as small pox island. Minicoy is in close vicinity to the Maldives, just separated by the 8 or Vangaaru channel and considered as an independent oceanic island not belonging to either Maldives or the Lakshadweep bank. The height of the island is around 1-2 m above the mean sea level (Basevi's account -1872), The livelihood of islanders depends largely on coconut plantation and fishing. Most of the young female habitants of the island work in ships and cargos as seamen.

History of Minicoy

Minicoy has more similarities to Maldives than to India culturally, geographically. It is just 125 km north of Maldives but 201 Km to South West of Kalpeni- nearest Indian Isle while 400 km west off the coast of Thiruvanathapuram. Though Minicoy people have affinity with Maldivians; their culture is an admixture of Maldives and Malabar.

There was strong trade and marriage bond between the Ali Rajas of Cannanore and the Sultan of Maldives. In 1734, after a cyclone, the islanders of Minicoy requested Maldivian King for financial support, but they got a refusal from the Maldivian King. Meanwhile, they found favour and support from the King of Cannanore- Ali Rajah and thus people of Minicoy obliged to the King of Cannanore and allied to his kingdom which included other islands of Lakshadweep.(Gabriel 1989). Thus the Minicoy culture assimilated elements of both Maldives and Malabar. After Independence, along with Laccadive and Aminidivi groups of islands, Minicoy too came under the Union Territory of Lakshadweep.

Islanders of Minicoy

Minicoy has older communities and a slightly varied class structure, having named land owners *Manikfan*, holding the same status as the Koyas ruling over the other class groups. *Thakrufan* are like Malmi, *Thakru* the sailors and *Raveris* – the landless nut plucking community like the Melacheris. As a deviation from the other islands the women of Minicoy enjoy special identification with specific names accorded to them.

Manikfan women are known as *Manika*, those belonging to the *Thakrufan* and Thakru are called *Beefanun and Bibees*, respectively and women of Raveris are known as Kambilo. This is also reflective of the social status awarded to the women, which despite the significant weakening elsewhere has held its position here. In fact, men from this island still settle with the women's family after marriage. The people speak a different tongue here – *Mahl*, although most can communicate in Hindi and Malayalam as well. The islanders of Minicoy dress differently too – men, apart from the high ranking *Manikfans* who prefer spotless white lungi, wear loosely tailored straight fit pants. The women wear a colourful long robe – libas, over a fitted bodice and cover their heads with a black scarf. Here, as opposed to the other islands, high ranking women are seen to wear gold, while the others prefer silver and black thread. With better earning among other classes, these differences are however on its way out. Also, traditional clothing is presently being replaced by modern garments – readily available to these seafaring people.

From available literature and interaction with the people during field study, it was found that Minicoy people are culturally akin to Maldives due to their strong resemblance to Malidivian Costumes, Script, and Language.

Physical Feature

Most of the islanders of Lakshadwep resemble people of Kerala while the islanders of Minicoy resemble primitive Simhalese. Their face is round and flat, modified to some extent by an admixture of Arab blood. The males are fair to dark complexion and flat waved to narrow waved hair and have medium stature. The females are found fairer in complexion than men.

Language

Mahl similar to Malidivian Divehi is the language spoken in Minicoy. It is written in a script named Thaana-akuru written right to left like Arabic and has words of Arabic, Sanskrit, Urdu origin.

Religion

More than 95% of the islanders are followers of Sunni Islam and they strictly obey the rules and laws of Islam (cf. Suad 2004; Gabriel 1989)

Education Scenario

Minicoy has population of 10,447 of which 5366 are males while 5081 females. (2011 census). Sex ratio is 947. Literacy rate of Minicoy is 82% out of which female literacy is about 80% and male literacy is around 84%.

The islanders are also found having a fair knowledge in few international languages as many of the males work as seamen in international ships and cargos and others come in contact with speech of people of these communities. Naturally the female members too are multilingual which makes them linguistically advanced than their other tribal peers.

Findings

Reasons for Women Empowerment in Minicoy

(a) Less Rigid Social Difference

Inhabitants were classified according to their wealth and jobs they used to do. The *Manikfan/Manika* used to be landlords and occupied the elite section of the society. Next to them in social status were the *Mallimin or Thakurfans,* sailors who mainly piloted sailing vessels during the ancient time. *Medukembin* or *Thakurus* were those who worked in boats during the sea trips. In between *Thakurfan and Thakuru* were the subclass known as Bebe. The Raveris were the labourers.Women corresponding to these four status grups were known as *Manikka, Berfan, Bebe and Kambilo* respectively. (Jha 1998).

According to their oral narratives and documents available on Minicoy,it was found that these 4 status groups correspond to those people who came along with 2 Maldivian princesses, *Kamboranin and Kohoratukamana*, to the island and their companions. When Male was invaded, the princesses were compelled to leave the place. These people replaced previous inhabitants of the island and became the ancestors of modern Minicoy islanders (Kattner 1996).

This social difference is not too rigid in Minicoy society, though different social classes exist. The difference is visible in dress pattern. Women of elite class prefer to wear dresses made up of Bengal Silk. Their Libas is a long silk dress with short sleeves, with openings only at the neck, where it is fastened together by 2 loops. Their head is covered by a scarf called Doli, worn in a particular manner. Both sexes are very fond of golden ornaments (Cotton 1995)

(b) Property Inheritance

The islanders are endogamous and live in the joint family so that brothers can retain their ancestral customs. Property is therefore inherited in the family line which is matriarchal. In recent years, a few cases of Exogamy were found when a male member married to a girl outside of the island. In such cases, their problems (if any) were discusses at a village meeting and resolved in a very amicable manner. Sometimes the relatives of the family would give a separate plot of land to them. Sometimes the married couple prefer to live in the mainland India as a solution to handle the situation, and they are deprived of the rights to ancestral property. The first police station of Lakshadweep was established in Minicoy but the crime rate in island, particularly among the native islanders is very negligible.

(c) Governance in the Island

Each household is presided over by the senior woman of the house, and in each house, an average of 6-7 people reside. Houses are grouped to form a village known as *Avah or Athiri.* There are 10 ancient *Avahs* presently in the island. There is no fixed population to form a village. Each *Avah* has a distinct colour for symbolic presentation of village identity and its own land, tuna fishing boat, country crafts and coconut trees. In each village there is *Athiri,* a common site at the western beach for boat landing. Income generated from the village property and their assets are used for the welfare of the village and the island. Common feasts and celebrations are organized at the village house which has a large hall and a larger space outside. They also play an important role in organizing awareness and other programmes.

2 Bodukakas (Headman) and 2 Bodudatha (Head Women), selected by the consensus of the villagers, rather than by election administer each *Avah.* The first *Bodukaka* looks after internal matters, and the second one deals with External affairs. Administration of male duties such as hauling the boats onshore, fishing, collection of boulders for safeguarding and marking the boundary of the village are also managed by them.

Each *Avah* has 2 village houses– one for male and the other for female. All the female duties beyond the family are normally carried out in the *Varhgange,* the female village house and male duties in the *Avarthuge,* male village house.

The Village Headmen and Headwomen, besides administering such activities as boat sailing, sanitation etc also monitor the income generation activities for their village and assign duties to the villagers on the matter of health and sanitation.

During the rainy season, the drainage of the village level gets blocked, and it is to be taken care of by the villagers and managed by *Bodudathas and Bodukakas. Bodudatha* monitors the proper disposal of tuna waste within the village area and manages religious festival like Eid and common feasts.

(d) Matriarchal Society

The responsibilities of family and society were taken care by female counterparts. Agriculture was not viable due to scarcity of land and other natural resources. Thus they developed a social norm in which they handed the social power to the female, who handled the responsibilities in their absence and managed the island society. In historical reports published by Ibn Batuta of 14th century, it is revealed that influence of women in Maldivian governance was strong (Reynolds 1975). Thus matrilineal norm existed even before their acceptance of Islam and it remained so after their conversion to Islam with their social custom ie Adat.

Challeneges Faced by the Tribal Women of Minicoy

(a) Lack of Higher Education

Though the literacy rate is comparatively higher than national average of 74.04%, interest in higher and technical education was found very low as they get job after obtaining education up to secondary level. Higher education among the female population is not encouraging as their education ends at higher secondary level at most of the times. Due to their traditional outlook, most females are not allowed to pursue higher education beyond the island. This is a barrier as higher education institutes are absent in Lakshadweep and they have to depend Kerala or other parts of India.

(b) Poor Connectivity

At many spots 4G mobile coverage is available in Lakshadweep islands, but Minicoy still suffers from poor connectivity. There are no film theatres and television remains the main source of entertainment which affects their exposure to global tastes and customs.

(c) Lack of Opportunities

Minicoy people are culturally linked to Maldivian people. But after 1956, the Indian Government has forbidden the direct travelling between the two islands despite their geographic and ethnographic similarities. Undoubtedly Minicoy people are thus unable to reap the opportunities in Maldives which is easier for than to fetch similar from Mainland India. Free people to people contact would have greatly benefitted the economy of Minicoy which is near to Maldives which is a world renowned tourism destination.

(d) Environmental Crisis

Raising ocean water levels due to global warming may eventually sink Minicoy under ocean. Thus every individual of Minicoy worries about their fate after some fifty odd years. Natural disasters especially during Monsoon often cut off Minicoy with rest of the world thus preventing any sort of transportation outside of the island.

Conclusion

Minicoy was under various rulers during various times until it became part of India. Influence of Modernization has their mark on livelihoods and thoughts. Yet they have preserved their ancestral culture and customs. They also give an example of real democracy not only at village level but also at the island as a whole. Even today, they obey the suggestions given by the village house as and when needed.

It is a matter of pride that male members identify themselves with their female counterparts. The positive administration of the female in all aspects proves that it is an inborn quality which has passed from one generation to the other. When rest of India is initiating various women empowerment programmes, the islanders demonstrate by retaining the value of women in the society more than men. Attacks against Women are so rare while their peers in India doesn't have the luck of Minicoy Women

The tribal people of Minicoy are ardent followers of Islam. Yet the adopted religious identity has not changed the core traditional practices like matrilineality and socio-political organization. Thus the tribal Women of Minicoy are model to every woman all over the world.

Acknowledgements

The author likes to express his heartiest thanks to the islanders and the resource persons of Minicoy. The deepest thanks go to Mr Raheem and Ms Sunaina of Minicoy for their voluntary time invested during field visit and continuous help whenever needed.

References

Basu, S.K., 1993. Health status of tribal women in India: educational implications. Social Change 23 (4).

Berreman, G.D., 1993. Sanskritization as female oppression in India. In: Miller, B.D. (Ed.), Sex and Gender Hierarchies. Cambridge University Press.

Census of India, 2001.

Census of India, 2011.

Chaudhuri, N.C., 1978. Womanhood in tribal India. In: Tribal Women in India. Indian Anthropological Society, Calcutta.

Davis, K., 1951. The Population of India and Pakistan. Princeton University Press, Princeton.

Dyson, T., Moore, M., 1983. On Kinship Structure, Female Autonomy, and Demographic Behavior in India. Population and Development Review 9 (1).

Elwin, V., 1961. Nagaland. Shillong: The Research Dept., Adviser's Secretariat. Ghurye, G.S., 1980. The Scheduled Tribes of India. Transaction Books, New Brunswick, NJ.

Kishor, S., 1993. May god give sons to all: gender and child mortality in India. American Sociological Review 58 (2).

Maharatna, A., 1998. On Tribal Fertility in the Late Nineteenth and Early Twentieth Century India, Working Paper Series No. 98.01, Harvard Center for Population and Development Studies, Harvard University.

Maharatna, A., 2000. Fertility, mortality and gender bias among tribal population: an Indian perspective. Social Science and Medicine, 50.

Maharatna, A., 2005. Demographic Perspectives on Indian Tribes. Oxford University Press.

Singh, K.S., 1994. The Scheduled Tribes. Oxford University Press.

Srinivas, M.N., 1977. The changing position of Indian women. Man 12

9

Women Empowerment: Opportunities and Challenges

— Dr. Prabudha S. Kamble

In the 21st Century, empowerment of women and children has become one of the most significant concerns. On contrary, in practical nature women empowerment is still an illusion. It is observed in the day to day life that women have become victimized by various social evils. Women Empowerment is the vital instrument to expand women's potentiality and ability to have resources and make strategic life choices and self-decisions. Empowerment of women is essentially in the process of upliftment of socio-economic and political welfare and development of women. The empowerment is safeguarding them against all forms of injustice and violence. The present study reveals that women of India are relatively disempowered and they enjoy somewhat lower status than that of men in spite of many government schemes plans and associations with non-governmental organizations. It is found that acceptance of unequal gender norms by women are still prevailing in the society. The study has focused the five dimensions of women's empowerment such as economic dimension, familial dimension, political dimension, social dimension and legal dimension. The different indicators of human development show that women have lesser access to property, resource, education, health facilities, medical care and lower percentage in earned income and finally lower participation in job market, if not least even in decision making power (World Bank, 2001).

Illiteracy is a social curse on human beings including the women. It adds impetus in the feminization of poverty and in deterioration in the status of women. India is not free from the curse of illiteracy. In 2001, the adult women literacy rate of India was only 42 percent whereas the adult male literacy rate was 67 percent. In term of enrollments in the educational institutions they are far below their male counterpart. The combined primary, secondary and tertiary enrollment ratio among female population in 2001 was only 49 percent whereas for male population it was 62 percent. The literacy gender parity index in India in 1995-1996 was only 0.8. At present 82 percent of male population aged seven year and above are literate, while 65 percent of the female are literate (Census, 2011). It is evident that male female gap in literacy has been declining during the era of globalization.

Women empowerment is the key factor to enable the decision-making power among women and also providing opportunities to prove their skills and talents to improve the societal development. However, reality is still averse due to the convention that in patriarchal society where in male persons enjoy the freedom of taking decisions in the matter of family and also social matter at the same time women only obey the decisions given patriarchal bent of mind.

Women are considerate as miserable in nature which disabled their ability to participate in the production process and also non-recognition of their housekeeping activities as productive in the family concern.

Globally, the gender gap in economic activity is very prominent. Women are, generally, unemployed and underemployed and when employed, in most of the cases, they are under paid and employed in informal sectors. Though working hour of women is very high within house, it is not counted as most of the time women are involved in household's jobs. These household's jobs are not included in economic activity of a country.

Economic Dimension

In the villages, women have control over their personal income and asset as it is a transparent and open society and access to household resources due to muscle power and legitimate relations. She also has freedom in choosing her occupation within the broad caste and religion limits. Women also decide about the small saving schemes in the villages in favor of children's future in most cases in consultation with her husband's only. In the case of buying and selling assets her husband is involved direct which is limiting her decision making power.

With the introduction of Self Help Group [SHG] in villages women are got more access to formal savings, insurance and low interest loan to start small enterprises. Their participation and involvement in the Gram Panchayat and SHG has gradually increased and also accessed to learning through proper training especially the tailoring programs. It is understood that in many cases, women are also threatened if widow and divorced.

The women play a vital role in economic field: as workers, consumers, entrepreneurs, managers and investors. In fact, across the world, including India, more women are employed but their share is still very low. Manufacturing work, traditionally a male preservation has declined, while jobs in services have expanded, reducing the demand for manual labor and putting the sexes on equal footing. It is observed that women are taking part in every field: architecture, lawyers, financial services, engineering, medical and IT jobs. They have also entered service occupations such as nurse, beautician, sales worker and waitress.

They are marching into domains which were previously reserved for males such as police, driver's army, pilots, chartered accoun-tants and commandos. In spite of their increasing number in every field, women still remain perhaps the world's most underutilized resources. Many are still excluded from paid work and many do not make best use of their skills. The rapid pace of economic development has increased the demand for educated female labor force almost in all fields. Women are earning as much as their husbands do, their employment nonetheless adds substantially to family and gives family an economic advantage over the family with only one breadwinner. This new phenomenon has also given economic power in the hands of women for which they were earlier totally dependent on males. Economic independent provides freedom and confident to take decisions in particularly in education and marriage.

Familial Dimension

In India, the customs of purdah (veil system), female infanticide, child marriage, sati system (self-immolation by the women with their husbands), dowry system and the state of permanent widowhood were both totally removed and checked to an appreciable extent after independence through legislative measures. Two Acts have also been enacted to emancipate women in India which are: protection of women from Domestic Violence Act, 2005 and the Compulsory Registration of Marriage Act, 2006. The Domestic Violence Act recognizes that abuse be physical as well as mental. It is found that girls' performance is increased in significant level at schools so as getting degrees and jobs in every field. There was a time when women's education was not a priority even among the elite. Since the last quarter of the 20th century and more so after the opening up of die economy, post-1991, a growing number of women have been entering into the economic field, seeking paid work (remunerative jobs) outside the family.

But the women belonging to poor families are unable to seek quality of education and education at all due to poverty. The finance and increased cost of education has left back the women deprived of education. The self-selection marriage is discouraged and is not honored by the family as well as community members but selection of life partner is encouraged if selection is done by elderly person. Articulation of personal problem to family members depended upon the relations between family members. Problems are shared with close family members only. The decision of educating the child is based on the financial condition and interest of the child to pursue education. The decisions about the health especially about the family planning are done by mother in law of the wife. In villages it is seen as improper and the norm does not permit to speak to a stranger, in such case even the neighbor has the right to interfere when she talks to strangers. The decision to immunize the child is taken by mothers and the decision is appreciated by family members and community members as well.

Woman feel inferior and takes away her self-respect is abuse. Compulsory Registration of Marriage Act could beneficial in preventing the abuse of institution of marriage and hindering social justice especially in relation to women. It helps the innumerable women in the country who get abandoned by their husbands and have no means of proving their marital status. It has helped in checking child marriages, polyandry and polygons marriages. It also enabled women to seek maintenance and custody of their children and widows claim inheritance rights. The Act is applicable on all women irrespective of caste, creed or religion. It provides empower Indian women to exercise their rights.

Political Dimension

In the villages, voting are done on the basis of different factors such as relative, community person, caste person, persons character, persons leadership quality, persons background of political power, his performance after once voted and elected, his ability to pay during elections, his/her favored by work performance. Voting is constituted by women as per the family decisions and the charisma of the contestant. She knows the name of the local leaders of panchayat and few state level elected leaders. Much involvement in political affairs is done by her husband though she is elected wherein she is slightly involved in day to day affairs of panchayat. With the introduction of SHG's women have developed the leadership qualities.

Social Dimension

Women is not supposed to move freely when she is newly married, but is allowed after getting two to three children. She is free to move outside her home when she works for family and along with peer groups. She also enjoys radio and television in free time. She is also free to talk. Now a day's educating girl is appreciated and welcomed in the family and household. Women now want the girl child also to earn after she grows up in a dignified manner as an educated person. Women feel inclusion of her participation in community level activities such as gram Saba, fairs, feasts, festivals and purchasing in weekly vegetable market. Consequently, women oppose the social curses such as Dowry system, Inter-caste marriage and preference of male child.

Legal Dimension

Most of the women do not know the mechanism of Justice used in the locality, women always feel that there is injustice and worse decisions, but her lead in the panchayat has changed her attitude and knowledge regarding the system. With the introduction of 33 percent reservation the attitude on reservation has changed as of now she easily complains about the deficiency of public services in her locality.

References

- Adhikary, M.L. and P. Dutta (2011), 'Factors Affecting Empowerment of Women: An Empirical Study in Burdwan, West Bengal', in Gender Deprivation and Empowerment of Women An

Indian Perspective, Utpal De and Bholanath Ghosh, (eds.) Lambert Academic Publishing, Germany, pp. 147-163.

- Adhikary, M.L. and P. Dutta, 'Women's Empowerment and Response towards Family Planning: Empirical Evidence from Bankura District, West Bengal', Asian Journal of Research in Business Economics and Management, Forthcoming.
- Ahmed, S., M.A. Keonig and R. Stephenson (2006), 'Effect of Domestic Violence on Prenatal and Early Childhood Mortality: Evidence from North India', American Journal of Public Health, Vol. 96(8), pp. 1423-1428. doi 10.2105/AJPH.2005.066316.
- Anuradha., P.S. (2012) 'An Empirical Study on Socio-Economic Empowerment of Women through Self-Help Groups', International Journal of Research in Commerce, Economics and Management, Vol. 2(1), pp. 84-86 Retrieved from www. ijrcm.org.in
- Dreze, J. and A. K. Sen (2002), 'India: Development and Participation', Oxford University Press, New Delhi.
- Government of India (2001), Census of India 2001, Ministry of Home Affairs, Office of the Registrar General and Census Commissioner, New Delhi.
- Government of India (2013), Annual Report 2012-13, Ministry of Women and Child Development.

10

Women Participation in Rotary Clubs

— Prof Dr. Shubhada Mohan Kulkarni

Introduction

In the modern era, empowerment is a multi-dimensional process which enables individuals and group of individuals to realize their full identity and powers in all spheres of life. According to Webster's dictionary the word empowerment indicates the situation of authority and to be authorized or to be powerful. Empowerment is a process that gives a person freedom in decision making (Kulkarni, 2017).

Women empowerment: means emancipation of women from the vicious grips of social, economical, political, caste and gender-based discrimination and granting freedom to make life choices. Women Empowerment itself elaborates that Social Rights, Political Rights, Economic stability, judicial strength and all other rights should be also equal to women. There is no discrimination between men and woman and equal opportunities and effective participation lead towards empowerment of women in all fields. This study is aimed to find out situation at Rotary international organization.

Rotary Club: an Introduction

Rotary is an international organization which was started in 1905 with vision of Paul Harris. At present, Rotary has

1.2 million members from all over the world. Rotary International supports Rotary clubs worldwide by coordinating global programs and initiatives. Rotary clubs unite dedicated people to exchange ideas, build relationships, and take action. Until 1989, the Constitution and Bylaws of Rotary International stated that Rotary club membership was for males only. Since then women become members and contribute in various capacities with the changing times, situations have changed for better, and women are holding key positions in this organization also but still there is scope for further improvement.

Women in Rotary club of Australia and New Zealand

Women in Rotary particularly in Australia and New Zealand were established in 2011 with the support and encouragement of the then Zone Director. The Core Essence of RI's Strategic Plan is a worldwide network of inspired individuals who translate their passions into relevant social causes to change lives in communities.

One of the key areas of this Plan is to Support and Strengthen Rotary Clubs by promoting diversity in membership and increasing member recruitment and retention. Rotary in Australia and New Zealand does not currently reflect, in its membership, the diversity of the communities in which it operates and serves. The role of Women in Rotary is to address one of the key areas of membership diversity, gender equity and work with Membership and Marketing and Public Relations Committees within Districts to develop plans that will increase membership and retention of women in Rotary and to support initiatives that promote female leaders at both Club and District levels.

Vision

To create and support a dynamic Rotary culture where men and women work together to expand and build on existing strengths with the benefits of diversity to improve the lives of individuals and communities in a way consistent with the RI Strategic Plan.

Core Value: Rotary provides opportunities for ordinary women to do extraordinary things

2016 Targets: 30 percent female membership in Australia and New Zealand, Gender balance in 20 percent of Clubs, 40 percent of District Board positions are held by women, Public image of Rotary within Australia and New Zealand reflects gender balance Plans and Programs developed for gender balance applied to other diversity initiatives

Implementation Strategies

- Increase recognition and retention of women in Rotary
- Rotary celebrating Women at International Women's Day Breakfast
- Increase Club, District and Public awareness of the opportunities, membership and benefits of women
- Presentations at Rotary Clubs, District Assembly PETS etc
- Develop resources for Clubs and Districts to support active involvement of women in Rotary
- Suggest projects that Clubs can embrace
- Women in Rotary is governed by an Executive Committee that meets to monitor strategy and put in place action plans

Strategic Plan 2016-2020- Targets

- 50 percent female membership in Australia and New Zealand
- 50 percent of all new members are women
- Gender balance in 40 percent of Clubs
- 50 percent of District Board & District committees positions are held by women

- 30 percent Club Presidents and Boards with a progressive increase of 5 percent
- Presidents understand Code of Conduct and responsibilities and they make sure the club understands these in terms of examples of accepted behaviour
- Public image of Rotary Clubs within Australia and New Zealand reflects gender balance and diversity
- Plans and programs developed for gender balance can be applied to connect with other diverse groups and Royce Abbey Champions of Change among men and women, young and old)

Implementation Strategy

Increase recognition and retention of women in Rotary

- Showcase Rotary celebrating Women at International Women's Day Breakfast and promote achievements of women led projects/ programmes
- Partner with local Government events and provide speakers/panelists
- Encourage cluster/clubs to hold "round table" discussions
- Hold "women at work" panel night for VCE students in local area to promote what women can achieve in the workforce and in the community
- Champions of Change speak at local events.
- Encourage women to take on leadership roles at all levels of Rotary and in the wider community by providing support and opportunities
- Encourage all 23 Rotary Districts in Australia (plus x in NZ) District Membership committees to have a woman "champion" Women in Rotary to identify how women can help, be involved and to use their expertise

- Increase Club, District and Public awareness of the opportunities, membership and benefits of women
- Presentation and initiatives at Rotary Clubs, District Assembly PETS etc
- Champion of Change recognition: DG changeover; Conference; Breakfast
- Select Male Rotarians, as WIR Male Champions of Change – to help endorse the acceptance of women Rotarians and in leadership roles
- Code of Conduct discussions being introduced into presidents training through Julie Mason and encouraged at all levels. Ensure following DG's and DGE's are involved in this process by (attending PETS and District Assemblies)
- Develop resources for Clubs and Districts (and Rotary AU office in Parramatta) to support active involvement of women in Rotary

Suggest projects that Clubs embrace

- Suggest how District and District Committees can embrace (or encourage) participation
- Videos produced by Wendy Gabriot to be shown at public community events
- Ensure all District PR People/teams promote the Wendy G videos within Rotary and to the wider community
- Social Media and broader media include content based on focus group
- Rotary Women make a difference strategy for Facebook
- Opportunities that women bring to clubs; women will bring other women
- Include content that is gained by focus groups
- Rotary media to ensure women are represented as significant participants

- Women in Rotary is governed by an Executive Committee that meets to monitor strategy and put in place action plans

Objectives of the Study

1. To find out current situation of women in Rotary
2. To understand perception about women contribution in Rotary

Research Design

The researcher has undertaken an exploratory study to find out perceptions regarding women in Rotary. The present study is a descriptive study and the primary data was collected by using of questionnaire and results of data analyzed throw light on the current scenario in Maharashtra, which represents a larger majority. The secondary data was also used to understand the background and developments over a period of time.

Data Analysis

For the study, 54 samples have collected by using of google form. The questionnaire [google form online questions] was used for data collection from the respondents. The questionnaire was sent to the respondents through email and social media

Major findings of the study: Demographic Analysis

- The study found that a majority of the respondents [56%] were male respondents
- A significant proportion of respondents belonged to the age [40.7%] category of 31-50, followed 51-65 years [15%].
- A significant level of respondents [48%] belonged to annual income was 10 lakh Rs-followed by [39%] 10-20 and [7.5%] belonged to 20-40 lakh.
- It if found that 37 percent of the respondents were post graduate, followed by 33.3 percent having

professional qualifications, 24 percent were graduate and only a few of the respondents 5.6 percent were having education upto graduation.

- The 31.7 percent respondents were from professionals and businessmen class each, followed by service 13 percent and industrialist by 7.5 percent.

Rotary connection

- All respondents were aware about Rotary International organization.
- The study found that 83 percent of the respondents were Rotarians such as members of Rotary club, 4 percent each were past members of Rotary and Inner wheel club
- The study findings revealed that 41 percent of the respondents are Rotarians have taken part in more than 10 years, followed by 37 percent are from 3-10 years, 15 percent from 1-3 years and 6 percent since last year. It means most of the respondents have long association with the organization.
- The entire women [100%] respondents were aware that women become member of Rotary.
- The study found that District Governor of Rotary District, president of Rotary Club, President Elect of Rotary Club and Rotary Anns have participated in the survey
- The study observed that 18 respondents (33.3%) were members of Board of Directors of their respective Rotary Clubs, followed by 17 respondents (31.5%) were office bearers in the Rotary District.
- 17 respondents (31.5%) were Chairman of Committees in the Club, 15 respondents (27.8%) were presidents of Rotary Club and 9 each (16.7%) were Club Secretaries and members of various

committees in the Rotary Clubs. This means they are familiar with the organization and their opinion is based on experience.

Opinions and perceptions

- The study found that 96.3 percent of the respondents agreed that they have lady rotary members
- The majority of the respondents (61%) opinioned that women members in their rotary club was upto 10 percent, followed by 26 percent respondents where membership is between 10-25 percent only 4 (7.5%) respondents said it is between 25-50 percent and 3 (5.6%) respondents mentioned their women membership is more than 50 percent
- The study found that ideal percent of women members in the club; considerable proportion of the respondents (39%) opinioned that there should be no limit, followed by 31.5% respondent preferring 50 percent members and 24 percent considering 40 percent as suitable number. Only 3 (5.6%) respondents felt that 20 percent is ideal representation of women in rotary club.
- A large spectrum of (96.3%) respondents felt women in rotary to be active only one exceptional respondent does not agree and one is not sure about activeness of women in rotary.
- A large majority of respondents (77.8%) believed that women get proper representation in rotary, whereas 14.8 percent do not agree that it is proper and 7.4 percent representatives are unsure about it.
- The study found that opinion about women getting high position in rotary is negative of 13 percent respondents, equal number of respondents is not sure about it and 74 percent accept that women do get high positions in rotary club and opinion

about women getting equal opportunities in Rotary is slightly different and better. 77.8 percent are positive, 9.3 percent negative and 13 percent are not sure about it.

- The study observed that a majority of (96.3%) respondents agree that women are respected in Rotary on 2 (3.7%) respondents consider that women are somewhat respected.
- The study found that opinions of respondents regarding women getting special privileges in rotary are almost equally divided. 24.1 percent respondents each believe in it being negative and not sure, where as 22.2 percent respondents said that they don't know and slightly more that 29.6 percent respondents were positive about it.
- The study corroborated that clubs conduct special activities for women, a vast majority of 81.5 percent respondents said yes and only 13 percent respondents said no to this question. Only 5.6 percent of the respondents were unsure about it.
- A large spectrum of (92.6%) the respondents were positive that they recommend women to join rotary. Only a few of 4(7.4%) the respondents were not sure.
- A majority of (85.2%) the respondents found contribution of women significant in rotary, followed by (11,1%) were not sure about it and only 2 (3.7%) respondents do not find women contribution significant in rotary.

Suggestions

- More involvement with authorities delegated.
- More representation should be given in District and Conference.
- Women Health, Social and Financial issues can be tackled by women so they should join Rotary. Adopt some reservation.

- All women must participate in all activities.
- Women must be given more administrative responsibilities and executive posts in the clubs.
- More Opportunities should be given for to show their ability and knowledge and provide responsibility.
- More responsibility should be given to women Rotarians to generate special projects for underprivileged women.
- The more percent in total should be increased.
- More number of female Rotarians should be increase.
- Male Rotarians should be women friendly and have strong belief in them and their ability to grant her leadership opportunities for her skills and of course men are set his Mind to accept her without hesitation.
- Woman should be given more opportunities in the day to day working of the club as well as in the district.
- They should be given equal opportunities for forming sub committees of Lady Anns to take initiative on family and kids gathering in enhancing fellowship.
- Improve the women's role in Rotary. Improve strength of women in Rotary club. Women in Rotary are doing wonderful job so as encouragement is needed to take new challenges, involvement in selection of leaders on district, international levels is required and help in implementation of their ideas with broader sense is needed.

Conclusion

The study has concluded that women enables their empowerment through taking part in rotary clubs and also trains to become the leader to improve the welfare of the women in all sphere of socio-economic, political and cultural development. The Rotary club is the key elements to improve the standard of life and livelihood opportunities of women so as it the enabler of women empowerment more vigorously in the area of skills and knowledge. In rotary club the women have actively participated and contributed significantly and proven their capacity, whenever and wherever chance is given so that women involvement is a key for the success of the overall development of the nation in this context rotary club provides opportunities to work world wide for the welfare and development of the women and protect their rights by providing proper awareness and training.

References

- Kulkarni, D. S. (2017). Women Empowerment in 21st Century. *Liberalization, Privatization and Globalization: Impact on Indian System-An Assessment* (pp. 156-160). Dhule: Ajanta Prakashan.
- Strategic Plan 2011-2016 (https://rotarywomen.org.au/web/wp)
- https://www.rotary.org/en/about-rotary/our-structure
- https://rotarywomen.org.au/about-us/

11

Issues and Challenges faced by Working Women

—V. Vijaya Lakshmi

Abstract

"Any woman who understands the problems of running a home will be nearer to understanding the problems of running a country." – MARGARET THATCHER

India is a traditional country and there is diversity in religions, culture and customs. Role of the women in India mostly is household and limited to domestic issues. India today has reached the zenith of success in many fields like science and technology, literature, movies and much more. Undoubtedly, without the active participation of women in national activities, the social, economic or political progress of a country will deteriorate and become stagnant; they work as lawyers, nurses, doctors, social workers, teachers, secretaries, managers etc. The women's contribution to the country's development is equal to that of their male counterpart. There is no profession today where women are not employed; still they experience a number of limitations that restrain them from comprehending their potential for expansion. Society has started seeing women in a different perspective. For centuries, women have been subjected to exploitation and torture, physically, sexually and mentally. Majority of the women still face discrimination and gender bias, in the last few decades, however, it is true that working women have to face problems by virtue of their sex. There are innumerable challenge and problems faced by them both at home and workplace, it was against this background that the government's all over the world felt the need to prioritize the interests of women and their participation at every stage of the development process. However, some issues are still prevalent in the country and more prominently in the rural India.

Rural India is the actual soul of the country where a maximum of its population resides yet it is also the most neglected and ignored by the Government. Rural and Urban Indian Women are facing many problems.

Keywords: *Women, Workplace environment, Challenges, Harassment, Suggestions*

Introduction

A working person of today may belong to the middle, lower or higher echelons of society. Working women of middle or lower class have the work for economic reasons while those belonging to the higher class work to time pass. The woman who works for financial reasons has to face many problems. Hard working she might be in her work, there are people ready to find faults in her work in order to harass her if she does not submit to their lewd advances. In addition, the poor woman cannot report against these people for fear of losing her job or her reputation in the eyes of colleagues, family or society.

Traditionally Indian women had been home makers but in the recent decades, proper education and better awareness, in addition to the ever increasing cost of living has made them to go outand choose careers. The number of working women is increasing day by day in India and different age group of working women both married and unmarried have faced different kinds of challenges and harassments in the workplace for being women. Most of the cases, they are facing personal, power and psychological harassment and they are suffering from mental and physical stress, depression, lack of confidence and lack of proper balance between employment and family care[1].

Being a working woman in the Indian context is not an easygoing task. Women literally have to face many outcomes of the social and the psychological ethos of the society and the people. They must have to maintain a balance between their families and career if they truly do not want to slaughter their aspirations and dreams to achieve independence and success in their lives. Moreover, in this hassle and bustle women get restless. They try to increase the working power for which they are constantly working that further makes them lacking in sleep. Gradually they feel frustrated and helpless because they see no one to help and support them. They sometimes tend to feel isolated, and then they invite many emotional and psychological problems. Insomnia and depression are two major mental problems Indian working women usually being noticed to suffer with. They feel an immense lack of Personal Space. Their whole time remains not theirs at all. They feel unable to share their feelings with anyone because they know that no one will understand them. Under this psychological pressure at a point of time, they are left with only two options, either to give up the job or to accept the depression as a part of their working life[2].

Women are not given first priority in social and economic decisions in her own family. According to United Nations Development Programmer (UNDP) report, women are involved in doing 67% work of world; still they are socially and economically deprived. They are receiving only 10% of the universal income and have 1% part in global assets. This discrimination also persists in their work place in unorganized sector. In informal sector, women workers do not get same wages for same nature of work for same hours done by men. They are exploited at workplace[3].

Discrimination at Workplace Today there is no field where the women have not shown their worth. From holding highest public office in bureaucracy to holding highest political position, the women have shouldered all kinds of responsibilities with grand success. However, Indian working women still face barefaced discernment at their workplaces. A major problem faced by the working women are Gender Bias, mental or physical harassment, Unequal Pay, Leadership, etc. at the work place. Even if to choose in study women facing problems, other are suggested that some particular line is better for women and they are forced to do that. Some of the fields like civil, mechanical, electrical, transportation are restricted for women and even if she chooses that field, mostly they feel strange or get some unexpected experience. Because of this, it may be possible that some particular area has more competition in getting job for women. Majority of working women continue to be denied their right to equal pay, under the Equal Remuneration Act, 1976 and are underpaid in comparison to their male colleagues.[4]

Women in the Workplace

Women in the workforce earning wages or a salary are part of a modern phenomenon, one that developed at the same time as the growth of paid employment for men; yet women have been challenged by inequality in the workforce. A woman is a social animal. To keep her in captivity, without access to work or finance or interaction with the outside world, is less than fair. Economic, social and political empowerment of women is essential for the development of any society. Working women are essential for the development of the society, so empowerment of women is important to the process of upliftment of economic, social, political status of women[5].

Balancing Personal and Professional Life

It is actually a very big challenge for the Indian working women to maintain a balance between their work and family. There are so many expectations of the family members and particularly from the kids. Since in India, women are primarily supposed to look after their families and kids, hence the family members generally perceive their career and professional aspirations as secondary and sometimes unessential. In majority of the families, there is a lack of emotional and moral support given to the women. In addition, there are many official expectations that the women have to fulfill otherwise it is very easy to terminate and hire any new woman personnel. In Indian families, women are already burdened with social and psychological ideologies of family members, which 'Expect' them to be all-rounder and perfect in all tasks and activities. In addition, it is a long age concept of the Indian society that the prime responsibility of a woman is to take care of her family and to become a perfect mother and a wife[6].

There are various issues and problems, which working people generally face in the society in India. Some of the problems are:

Mental harassment

Mental harassment at work is often a form of workplace bullying. The Workplace Bullying Institute defines the phenomenon as verbal abuse, threatening, humiliating or intimidating offensive behaviors, and conduct that stops you from doing your work. In India, 53% of working women said they would likely speak out and report harassment. Women leaders have to face many work issues like offensive comments, threats to sexual assaults and other sexual advantages. Women feel insecure in going to office under such circumstances. Negative consequences of such harassment are usually worse leading to a downfall in leadership.

One more interesting, fact that female colleagues also give mental stress, like indulging in jealous behavior, unnecessary gossip and rivalry. Several women also faced injustice by their female colleagues where they spread negative rumors about one's character and upbringing. They try to harass by creating confusion and misunderstanding with superiors and complain about other females[7].

Sexual harassment:

Women not only in the workplace but also outside the workplace face sexual harassment. They have a fear of sexual abuse like touching, staring, lewd comments etc. At present, almost all working women are prone to sexual harassment irrespective of their status, personal characteristics and the types of their employment. They face sexual harassment on way on transports, at working places, educational institutions and hospitals, at home and even in police stations when they go to file complaints. Even the law protectors are also violating and outraging modesty of women[8]. The major area where women have been affected in the workplace is sexual harassment. The men are in an immediate supervisory position, which gives them an opportunity to exploit their subordinate women. Sexual harassment is closely linked to sex discrimination. Sexual discrimination forces women into lower paying jobs, and sexual harassment helps keep them there. Whether the problem is sexual harassment or sexual discrimination the problem continues to exist in the workplace, creating tension that make their jobs more difficult.

Gender Discrimination at Workplace:

Gender bias is another challenge that many women experience at their work place. Women are considered as weaker section of the society than men consider and given less importance. Gender discrimination affects women in the areas like nutrition, education, health, care, decline of female population, job, public life, etc.[9] The profession of teachers, nurses, gynecologists (doctors), secretaries, desk- managers or counselors are easily recruited to Indian women and taken as among the most suitable jobs for Indian women whereas jobs like of a manager, engineer, geologists, Para-military, administrators and other dignified jobs are primarily recruited to males of equivalent qualifications. They are often deprived of promotions and growth opportunities at work places but this does not apply to all working women. A majority of working women continues to be denied their right to equal pay. The Equal Remuneration Act 1976, professes equality in remunerations but it has seldom been exercised in fact Indian working women are usually underpaid. The preconceived notion that the women are less capable of working hard in comparison to their male counterparts has deeply affected the salaries or wages given to the women in India. Usually the women, who work in Indian factories and labor-oriented places, are generally paid lesser in comparison to their male colleagues. One must understand that women are blessed with the opportunity to bring another soul into this world and this factor must not be a hindrance for their growth and progress. It is a promising change to see that many social welfare organizations like the UN are raising this concern globally and is pledging to remove gender bias in workplace.

Lack of proper Family Support

Lack of proper family support is another issue that working women suffers from. At times, the family does not support women to leave the household work and go to office. They also resist for women working until late in office which also hampers the performance of the women and this affects their mental, physical health and dissatisfaction with life in general and with family life promotion. The role of women in the family and in the community has changed significantly in the past two decades. Women have to balance between their professional and personal time. They have to learn how to work in the most efficient and effective ways and manage their priority well. Therefore, they would not have to spend such a long hours at work and could give more time for their family, if women could manage their schedule and priority well they could be successful working women and homemakers well. It is a big challenge for women to balance these two things and adjust priorities[10].

No Safety of Working Women

The most threatening challenge for women at work place is their security. With more and more cases of physical assault and abuse being reported in dailies and news channels. In some families, it may not be acceptable to work after six o' clock. Those families that do accept these working hours may experience considerable anxiety every day about a woman's safety while traveling. So many issues affect a working woman because she is closely protected or watched by her family and the society. Many organizations have employed special security services for helping their women employees to get back home at late nights. Not just working women but every girl should always be prepared to face the wrath of uncivilized men and hence must equip themselves with defense mechanism and face their challenge with oozing self-confidence.

Maternity Leaves

Insufficient maternity leave is another major issue faced by a working mother. This not only affects the performance of women employees at work, but also detrimental to their personal lives. Most of the firms have policies where maternity leaves are granted for the first two babies, which is appreciable. However, once the woman resumes office post her maternity break, she may be in for surprise as her role would no more be the same. She may have to begin from beginning all over again. To bridge this gap and ease the challenge, corporate firms have now included flexibility policies for women who resume their career post maternity breaks.[11]

Workplace Adjustment

Working women's adjustment problems depend upon their emotional intelligence. Adjusting to the workplace culture, whether in a new company or not, can be intensely stressful, more particularly their adjustment is related to self-regard, interpersonal relationship, impulse control, problem solving, emotional self-awareness, flexibility, reality testing, stress tolerance, assertiveness and empathy. Maladjustments to workplace cultures may lead to subtle conflicts with colleagues or even with superiors. In many cases, office politics or gossips can be major stress inducers[12].

Indian working women are truly living a challenging life where they encounter with many hurdles, social and psychological pressure of the people around them. A woman fully deserves respect, support, compassion and empathy, from her family and kids. When she is devotedly doing everything for her family then at least she should be rewarded with emotional and moral support. All she wants a little concern, respect and affection. The Laws should be practiced strictly, which provide total security, equal remuneration and a safe working atmosphere for the working women. There is a deliberate need to reshuffle the mindsets and beliefs of the family members, employers, colleagues and the public at large.[13] Educated urban women are presumed to be more aware of the opportunities and challenges of the workplace or educated urban women can better understand their roles and limitations in the workplaces and are perceived to be bold enough to develop their own personalities, with or without encouragement from their families.[14]

Conclusion

In a patriarchal society like India, a particular boundary exists only for women, and if they try to cross that boundary then people start maligning them. Traditionally people think that men should only work and gain money and women should work as house hold, but the financial demands on the Indian families are increasing that's why women also should company in gaining income for families. Working women's are contributing a lot in the economic growth and a large part of economic activities are undertaken by women and overwhelmingly this working women faced a lot of challenges at their working place. The different age group of working women both married and unmarried have faced different kinds of challenges and harassments in the workplace for being women. Most of the cases, they are facing personal, power and psychological harassment and they are suffering from mental and physical stress, depression, lack of confidence and lack of proper balance between employment and family care. Women workers are often subject to sexual harassment, the sexual harassment by male colleagues is a reality. Mental harassment by female colleagues is also a reality. Women have different perception of their needs, fears, frustrations etc. Some are happy with their jobs; some are frustrated because of harassment, both mental and physical; some women have a good job environment; some are highly depressed because of issues with their colleagues, both male and female. Some women have a good job environment; some are highly depressed because of issues with their colleagues, both male and female. Therefore, a fundamental change is required in attitudes of employees, family members and public.

Notes

1. https://www.researchgate.net/publication/329252767
2. http://www.proud2bindian.com/society/challenges-faced-by-working-women-in-india/
3. http://www.nevillewadia.com/images/Cronicle2015/Azadeh-Barati15.pdf
4. Dr. Kamini B. Dashora , "Problems Faced By Working Women In India" International Journal of Advanced Research in Management and Social Sciences, ISSN: 2278-6236
5. IJCRT1703087 International Journal of Creative Research Thoughts (IJCRT) pg. 625
6. http://www.proud2bindian.com/society/challenges-faced-by-working-women-in-india/
7. http://ethesis.nitrkl.ac.in/6094/1/E-208.pdf
8. http://www.nevillewadia.com/images/Cronicle2015/Azadeh-Barati15.pdf
9. https://www.indiacelebrating.com/essay/issues-and-problems-faced-by-women-in-india-essay/
10. https://www.researchgate.net/publication/292975400_WORK_-FAMILY_BALANCE_-A_CHALLENGE_FOR_A_WOMEN
11. https://content.wisestep.com/women-in-the-workplace/

12. http://www.vinayakamission.com/userfiles/phd/O746500002.pdf
13. http://www.hindu.com/mp/2007/03/08/images/2007030800730101.jpg
14. https://www.researchgate.net/publication/329252767

12

Women and Livelihood Security Through Mgnrega: Experiences from South India

—Dr. Anji. A &
Dr. J. Balamurugan

Introduction

The Indian Government implements various programmes to improve the livelihood opportunities at grassroots level. Subsequently, the Mahatma Gandhi National Rural Employment Guarantee Act (MGNREGA) 2005 is implemented in order to improve the socio-economic condition at rural level. The MGNREGA main aim is to provide the social and economic development for rural people, especially to bring out the sustained improvement in their living condition through reasonable income for accessing the social goods.

The status of women is intimately connected with their economic status and opportunity for the participation in economic activities. In this context, the MGNREGA enables their livelihood security in rural areas by providing at least 100 days of guaranteed wage employment in a financial year to every household whose adult members volunteer to do unskilled manual work.

Plethora of research studies revealed that programmes have major impact on rural area, present study outlined the performance of the Mahatma Gandhi National Rural Employment Guarantee Scheme (MNREGS) in Tamil Nadu.

The present study has understood that gender an analytical lens to view a social construction as well as socialization process that is recursive and recasts the being and becoming of persons into men and women. These men and women perform socially normative functions and roles in a society they possibly transform. In the term, the notions of the society pre-determine the growth and development of persons. These notions are constructed socially and hence gender is a social construction and this includes the processes of growing up socialization. Thus, social construction and socialization make up the identities and social behaviours of being men and women.

In general, gender is reduced to understand men and women as social categories; it is not limited to the being and becoming of men and women alone but includes a diversity of identity and preference.

In the process of socialization, gender systematically entrenches discourses of power and powerlessness, in the growing person and thereafter, this discourse perpetuates within interpersonal, family, social and cultural systems.

To understand gender is practiced of power and thereby transform them towards empowerment and equality. As rights based legislation, MGNREGA has recognized the imperatives of gender empowerment as well as equality in its design features. There is a view that MGNREGA is a unique Act because it is gender sensitive in its formulation. Other public work sites such as brick kilns or quarries, stone chipping or industrial projects are singularly unfriendly to women, especially to rural women. Other provisions are part of the policy and implementation of MGNREGA. Several states with strong women's Self-Help Group [SHG] networks have used these design features of MGNREGA and worked for its strong implementation in their states.

The federations of SHG women leaders have looked at the larger gender empowerment project and reframed the political participation of women in their local contexts as well as engaged in ensuring accountability within MGNREGA. In this background, it is surprising that there are not many questions and doubts relating to MGNREGA and gender in public discourse. This is particularly curious since the participation of women in this scheme has been impressive. Further, states such as Tamil Nadu have gender and disability friendly and the participation of elderly in MGNREGA has also been impressive.

Hence, this paper focuses on assessment of MGNREGA, on women's labour participation literacy, health, sanitation and their security issues. The findings of the study suggest that, women got financial security along with livelihood social security through MGNREGA. The analysis puts forward key issues that merit serious consideration as well as the major recommendations. This study based on secondary data collection from the evaluation studies of MGNREGA conducted two south Indian states.

Table 1: MGNREGA and Women's Participation across States

S.No	*State*	*Percentage of Women Person Days*	
		2013-14	214-15
1	Andhra Pradesh	58.68	58.72
2	Arunachal Pradesh	30.35	30.21
3	Assam 26.01	24.75	28.19
4	Bihar	34.97	37.17
5	Chhattisgarh	48.53	49.87
6	Gujarat	43.96	43.24
7	Haryana	41.71	41.66
8	Himachal Pradesh	62.52	61.04
9	Jammu And Kashmir	23.15	25.38
10	Jharkhand	31.89	32.06

(*Contd...*)

11	Karnataka	46.59	46.86
12	Kerala	93.37	92.17
13	Madhya Pradesh	42.65	43.22
14	Maharashtra	43.69	43.47
15	Manipur	35.25	38.27
16	Meghalaya	41.62	42.57
17	Mizoram	30.20	40.27
18	Nagaland	28.93	31.28
19	Odisha	33.57	33.79
20	Punjab	52.74	57.43
21	Rajasthan	67.76	68.26
22	Sikkim	44.85	48.18
23	Tamil Nadu	83.94	85.42
24	Telangana		61.07
25	Tripura	47.11	49.36
26	Uttar Pradesh	22.17	24.75
27	Uttarakhand	44.88	50.56
28	West Bengal	35.55	41.37
29	Andaman And Nicobar	47.18	50.44
30	Dadra & Nagar	NR	NR
31	Daman & Diu	NR	NR
32	Goa	75.30	74.88
33	Lakshadweep	22.50	36.59
34	Puducherry	85.65	86.29
35	Chandigarh	NR	NR
	Total	**52.80**	**54.86**

The women's participation in the scheme is higher than the mandatory 33 per cent; it was 54.86 per cent up to 2015. At a disaggregated state level, women's participation varies across states with Kerala, Goa and Tamil Nadu showing higher women's participation. Andhra Pradesh and Himachal have shown high participation.

States such as Uttar Pradesh show very low women's participation as do the North Eastern states and Jammu and Kashmir. The quick preliminary check crosses validate the sex ratios in the states with high women's participation rates. According to Census 2011, the top five states with healthy sex ratios are Kerala, Puducherry, Tamil Nadu, Andhra Pradesh and Chhattisgarh. It is seen that Goa, Kerala, Tamil Nadu and Puducherry compare well in terms of their sex ratios and participation of women. At the lower level, the situation is more complex with some of the states with low women's participation rates along with being states with lower women's literacy rates such as Uttar Pradesh and skewed sex ratio's such as Haryana. These states show that articulate picture of the challenges that women face including participating in MGNREGA works.

It is seen that high women's participation rates in MGNREGS, women's literacy rates and sex ratios are concurrent in the high performing states, while this may not be so equivocal and linear in other states. A detailed analysis is beyond the scope of this document, still clearly this brief attempt implies two things, one that some states may show a higher unity on several genders empowerment related parameters and high women's participation in MGNREGA is certainly one of the important parameters in this assessment. In other states the complexities of negotiation and confrontation for gender empowerment may show differential effects.

Market Wages and Conditions on Work Sites

The women are entitled to equal wages in MGNREGA which is a key to the project of gender empowerment. Through the MGNREGA wage parity is achieving. At present, different states have wage rates ranging from Rs 150–205. Many research have conducted prior to 2012 addressed queries relating to wage parity are analyzed in Sameeksha I. Further, research questions on changes in rural labour markets and women are addressed by Mihir Shah (ed.) (2012), *MGNREGA Sameeksha: An Anthology of Research Studies on the Mahatma Gandhi National Rural Employment Guarantee Act 2005, 2006-2012.* A few research studies wages for work with private employers and contractors are higher than wages under MGNREGA and this issue recurs particularly across several fast urbanizing blocks across the country.

These fast urbanizing blocks present a situation where local men may prefer to work in these industrial and infrastructure projects, while local women work with MGNREGA.

The research on intra-household decision making reveals a picture where men typically migrate and look for industrial and infrastructure labour work. Pellissery and Jalan (2011) show that, 'men typically have a lump sum earning' in their heuristic, whereas MGNREGA work comes with 'small sums'. Therefore, women are preferred for MGNREGA work within households.

Women internalize as their day to day functionality is constrained by small cash requirements which is covered by MGNREGA in these days which need to negotiate and re-negotiate with male members in their households as well as in work social spaces. This relates to a term coined by feminists and gender activists on the linkages between gender and poverty 'feminization of poverty'. Feminization of poverty encapsulates several ideas, one of which is a renegotiation of a lower power relation so that women continue and remain poor. It appears women work in MGNREGA and settle down for a partial empowerment at grassroots level.

This appears to the case for elderly men, who again are socially powerless and may again need small amounts of cash for their day to day needs. The household decision of a man working for better wages while a woman works in MGNREGA being economically rational and looked at as a replacement of patriarchal power relations as MGNREGA evolves, there is a need to locate and re-locate its impact within the larger project of gender empowerment. This scheme acknowledges decent working conditions on the work site. However, research shows that provisions of decent work, especially for women and children needs to be implemented uniformly across states.

In a study on women workers in Assam, Bhattacharya and Vaquoline (2013) present a feminist conceptual framework on the idea of power. Since power implies agency, power in a feminist perspective implies 'power to act' this is in contrast to the power in hierarchies, where it implies 'power over' resources and people. The current research found women reporting better decision making that the conditions on work sites continued to challenge women workers. More importantly, research by Narayanan and Das (2014) identified the difficulties experienced by vulnerable groups of women headed households, single women and elderly women. Vulnerable groups of poor women represent a double hazard and their needs and concerns are prioritized. Therefore, from a gender perspective, decent work implies the capacity to act freely and also conducive conditions on work sites such as provision for childcare, shade and medicines. These form a crucial link to women's agency and their capacity to act.

Research by Bhattacharya and Vaquoline (2013), Pellissery and Jalan (2011) as well as that by Narayanan and Das (2014) emphasized that type of work, perceptions of male workers about women and their work on site, gendered work loafing by men when women are present on the work site and the lack of adequate childcare facilities on work sites are the key issues that need to address.

Women and Financial Inclusion - Table: 2, Women Workers' Account for years 2014–15

Sl. No.	*State No. of*	*Beneficiary Workers with Accounts*	*No. of Women Beneficiary Workers with Accounts*	*% of Women Beneficiary Workers with Accounts*
1	Andhra Pradesh	8,082,172	4,102,454	50.76
2	Arunachal Pradesh	84,119,	27128	32.25
3	Assam	3,439,413	1,094,553	31.82
4	Bihar	5,427,926	1,986,870	36.60
5	Chhattisgarh	7,074,240	3,337,656	47.18
6	Goa	19,198	13,259	69.06
7	Gujarat	3,917,929	1,845,313	47.10
8	Haryana	1,002,084	410,819	41.00
9	Himachal Pradesh	1,013,446	535,929	52.88
10	Jammu And Kashmir	1,291,245	337,342	26.13

(*Contd...*)

11	Jharkhand	3,721,450	1,413,271	37.98
12	Karnataka	11,471,580	5,366,556	46.78
13	Kerala	2,500,748	1,983,906	79.33
14	Madhya Pradesh	11,928,104	5,421,164	45.45
15	Maharashtra	5,165,562	2,188,970	42.38
16	Manipur	304,150	157,311	51.72
17	Meghalaya	153,456	91,486	59.62
18	Mizoram	359,709	170,235	47.33
19	Nagaland	207	92	44.44
20	Odisha	6,769,475	2,848,891	42.08
21	Punjab	1,088,461	488,314	44.86
22	Rajasthan	11,120,501	6,109,465	54.94
23	Sikkim	105,192	49,183	46.76
24	Tamil Nadu	8,188,255	6,226,540	76.04
25	Telangana	2,780,320	1,490,366	53.60
26	Tripura	1,306,889	604,985	46.29
27	Uttar Pradesh	12,306,176	2,966,655	24.11
28	Uttarakhand	957,478	457,814	47.81
29	West Bengal	14,310,438	5,378,546	37.58
30	Andaman And Nicobar	13,033	6,725	51.60
31	Dadra & Nagar Haveli	2,190	1,884	86.03
32	Daman & Diu	0	0	0
33	Chandigarh	107	35	32.71
34	Lakshadweep	7,736	2,541	32.85
35	Puducherry	76,783	54,796	71.36
	Total	**125,989,772**	**57,171,054**	**45.38**

Economic empowerment and financial inclusion are crucial for gender empowerment and equality. This scheme has ensured that women are included in formal banking systems. Provisional data in the MGNREGA and Management Information System [MIS] show that women have access to accounts in individual names and joint names. More research needs to do for exploring the linkages between access to a formal financial system and access to formal credit, the preference for formal or informal credit by women and the initiating circumstances and changes in decision making by women in the households.

At present, women are able to utilize banking systems, micro ATMs, passbooks or these tasks are done by men in the households. Above table shows that, the number of women beneficiary accounts from administrative records. Women beneficiary accounts under MGNREGA are crucial and women access to a formal financial system might act as an enabler in any pro-women, pro-poor initiative. Self help groups in the southern states have taken leadership positions, starting from economic empowerment to leadership in larger social and political domains.

In general, positive results are substantiated through research done in the most vulnerable blocks in West Bengal, where women reported that their satisfaction of being able to spend on their expenses including for their children's health. This research pointed out that women are not part of the planning and social audit process as a key gap. As mentioned earlier, empowerment is understood as 'power to act' as opposed to hierarchy. The research revealed that, even as economic constraints lead women to demand work under MGNREGA and working in MGNREGA eases some of these constraints, several issues relating to their decision making power persist. However, the fact those women workers get their wages transferred directly to their individual and joint accounts in a positive indicator for women's empowerment.

Created Individual and Community Assets

The study has observed that lack of participation by women in the planning process has been one of the key gaps in MGNREGA's planning and the list of works for the labour budget. In a gendered analysis of worker participation in Andhra Pradesh, Pellissery and Jalan (2011) carried out primary fieldwork in 13 work sites in the state and found that lack of participation in the planning process has led to a perception of women as mere 'labouring hands' on work sites.

The research reports that even as legal provisions exist and MGNREGA is pro-empowerment in its design, the struggle for gender empowerment continues. However, importantly there were several positive reports by women, especially single women who if not for MGNREGA have had to bargain for wages with employers. Further, the study testimonies of women workers even though the work was hard, they satisfied and able to use the wages for children's needs. The qualitative testimonies suggest that needs of women workers, especially in women headed households within the rural contexts were being addressed, at least in a partial sense by the implementation of MGNREGA.

A very few research studies have been done the role of women in the planning of works either through the Gram Sabha and as Panchayats, even as unreliable records intuit women Panchayat presidents plans their works. The study suggests that women and men value work differently; with few researches reporting that men value works related to enhancing agricultural production while women value works relating to repairs of anganwadi buildings and healthcare. Beyond this stereotypical presentation, the direct and perceived utility of certain works ine more for women than for men. In recent years, there has been an increased focus on sanitation programmes and the Government of India has taken up the mission for an open defecation free area in India. Open defecation relates to health and hygiene in human development but more importantly relates to dignity of all men and women.

Apart from health and sanitation issues, recent incidents have brought out the issue of women's security and open defecation. In this context, it is notable that individual household toilet units have been a priority for work under MGNREGA under 'individual assets'. Whereas, the construction of Individual Household [IHHLs] was under convergence with National Bharath Abhiyan [NBA] earlier, as of now, this is done fully under MGNREGA. Further, there are inter-state variations with several states such as Karnataka, Andhra Pradesh, Madhya Pradesh and Tamil Nadu making concerted efforts to construct IHHLs under MGNREGA, while several states still lag behind in this. Sanitation, nutrition and stunting concerns and security of women are important issues and MGNREGA individual assets. MGNREGA potentially contributes towards these important human development concerns wherever they have been taken on as state policies and as individual initiatives.

Findings and Conclusions

- The study found that with high sex ratios are Kerala, Puducherry, Tamil Nadu, Andhra Pradesh and Chhattisgarh. It is observed that Goa, Kerala, Tamil Nadu and Puducherry compare well in terms of their sex ratios and participation of women. At the lower level, the situation is more complex with some of the states with low women's participation rates along with being states with lower women's literacy rates such as Uttar Pradesh and skewed sex ratio's in Haryana. These states show that articulate picture of the challenges that women face including participating in MGNREGA works.
- The study revealed that lack of women's participation in the planning process is a significant issue. This relates not just to the relevance and ownership of completing works and the selection of works but to accurate capture of demand and the utilization of the scheme by women who need it the most.
- The study observed that type of works taken up may not be amenable to the works that women can do and women also need decent work facilities including facilities for children.
- The study found that substantive participation of women in Gram Sabhas needs to assess that their contribution to decision making is mapped.
- The study revealed that participation of women in social audit Gram Sabhas over the years can reveal certain insights on women's empowerment.

Conclusion

Over the last few years researchers have turned their gaze at not just the direct effect of MGNREGS on economic indicators but on human development indicators as well. Poverty and deprivation are intricately linked to political and governance systems, health and education as well as other opportunities and freedoms that affect the capability of persons. Evidence shows that MGNREGA impacts some aspects of human capability. This research paper is evident and directed that needs more research effort to arrive at definitive conclusions while assessing the role of MGNREGA on human development indicators, especially women. It is important to note that plethora of research studies provide a quick assessment of the impact of MGNREGS wages on the livelihood security on women. However, the long-term impact as in the case of human development and livelihood security could assess by longitudinal studies that map the journey of a household over a period of time.

References

1. Bhattacharya, R. and P. Vaquoline (2013), 'A Mirage or a Rural Life Line? Analysing the impact of Mahatma Gandhi Rural Employment Guarantee Act on Women Beneficiaries of Assam', Space and Culture, India.
2. Coffey, D. (2013), 'Children's welfare and short-term migration from rural India', Journal of Development Studies 49 (8): 1101-117.
3. Das, Upasak (2014), 'Can the Rural employment Guarantee Scheme reduce the short term migration: Evidence from West Bengal, India', paper presented at the International Seminar on MGNREGA at Indira Gandhi Institute of Development Research (IGIDR).
4. Dr. K.V.S., Prasad. (2012). "Performance of Mahatma Gandhi National Rural Employment Guarantee Act (MGNREGA): An Overview", ISSN: 2230-9519.
5. Dr. Vilas M. Kadrolkar., (2012). "An Impact Assessment Study of Mahatma Gandhi National Rural Employment Guarantees Act' (MGNREGA) In Karnataka", Global Research Analysis, Volume 1, Issue 4, September 2012, ISSN No 2277-8160.

6. John, Papp and Imbert Clément (2014), Short-term migration and India's Employment Guarantee Scheme. Mumbai: Indira Gandhi Institute of Development Research.
7. Mihir Shah (ed.) (2012), MGNREGA Sameeksha: An Anthology of Research Studies on the Mahatma Gandhi National Rural Employment Guarantee Act, 2005. 2006-2012. New Delhi: Ministry of Rural Development, Government of India.
8. Narayanan, Sudha and Upasak Das (2014), 'Women Participation and Rationing in the Employment Gurantee Scheme', Economic and Political Weekly XLIX (46).
9. Pellissery, Sony and Sumit Kumar Jalan, Towards transformative social protection: a gendered analysis of the Employment guarantee act of India (MGNREGA). Anand: Institute of Rural Management (IRMA).
10. Shenbagaraj., P., and Arockiasamy., S., (2013). "Impact of MGNREGA on local development: A study of Ottapidaram blocks in Thoothukudi district, Tamil nadu", International Journal of Development Research Vol. 3, Issue, 04, pp.007-011, April, 2013.
11. Soumyendra, Kishore Datta and Krishna Singh. Poor, Women's Job Participation in and Efficiency of NREGA Program—Case Study of a District in India. Burdwan University.

13

Impact of Climate Change on Women, Gender Equality in Contemporary India: Issues and Challenges

— *V. Manjuvani*

"We are the first generation to be able to end poverty, and the last generation that can take steps to avoid the worst impacts of climate change. Future generations will judge us harshly if we fail to uphold our moral and historical responsibilities."

— Ban Ki-moon,
Former General Secretary, United Nations

Abstract

In the contemporary era, women are facing various issues and challenge particularly the gender bias. Moreover, the climatic changes are affecting the women more vulnerably. The detrimental effects of climate change felt in the short term through natural hazards such as landslides, floods, Tsunami and hurricanes and in the long-term, through more gradual degradation of the environment. The adverse effects are felt in many areas including in relation to inter alia agriculture and food security, biodiversity, ecosystems, water resources and human health.

In this scenario, women are more vulnerable to effects of climate change as they constitute the majority of the people in India are poor and dependant for their livelihood on natural resources that threatened by climate change. Furthermore, women face social economic and political barriers that limit their coping capacity. Women and men in India are depending upon natural resource for their livelihood. Those charged with the responsibility to secure water, food and fuel for cooking and heating face the great challenges and when coupled with unequal access to resources in decision making process, limited mobility places women are in a position where they are disproportionately affected by climate change. Thus important to identify gender- sensitive strategies to respond to environmental and humanitarian crisis caused by climate change.

The present study focuses on Proactive role in integrating a gender dimension into climate change issues and challenges which play, in terms of achieving development results that are sustainable to achieve climate related projects, which delivers in the ways to improve the respective capacities of men and women to respond and adopt the Impacts of climate change in their specific contexts and thus benefit from development progress.

Introduction

Gender impacts of climate change has been identified as an issue requiring greater attention by the Commission on the Status of Women (CSW)[1] Gender norms, roles and relations are key factors in determining vulnerability and adaptive capacity to health impacts of climate change. Women and men vulnerability is to impact of extreme climate events which is determined biology and differences in their social roles and responsibilities. Although they vary, these roles and responsibilities exist in all societies. The expectation from women to fulfill their roles and responsibilities as careers of their families often places extra burdens on them during extreme climate events. The expected role of men as economic providers for their families often places extra burdens on them in the aftermath of such events.

Definition of Gender and Gender equality: Gender describes the characteristics associated with being male or female. These attributes, opportunities and relationships are socially constructed and learned behaviours, influenced not only by biological sex, but predominantly by the society where live in. Gender is a part of the broader socio-cultural context and therefore varies over different cultures and time periods[2].

Gender equality refers the women and men have equal value, rights, and opportunities to participate in every aspect of life, at every level of society. Equality does not mean that men and women will become the same, but that women's and men's rights, responsibilities and opportunities will not depend on whether they are born male or female. Gender equality means that the interests, needs and priorities of both men and women are taken into consideration, recognizing the diversity of different groups of women and men.

Climate change: The definition adopted by the United Nations Framework Convention on Climate Change (UNFCCC), which defines "climate change" as "a change[3] of climate which is attributed directly or indirectly to human activity that alters the composition of the global atmosphere and which is in addition to natural climate variability observed over comparable time periods". In general, women are vulnerable to climate change because they are more prone to the adverse impacts from climate change.

Their limited adaptive capacities arise from prevailing social inequalities and ascribed social and economic roles that manifest itself in differences in property rights, access to information, lack of employment and in equal access to resources. Further, changes in the climate usually impacts on sectors are traditionally associated with women, such as paddy cultivation, cotton and tea plantations, and fishing. This means increased hardship for women. The plethora of studies show that climate change has an adverse impact on fishing, as the sea level rises and saline water enters into freshwater systems, making fishing difficult. Further, in extreme events more women deaths are observed for women's inability to swim or run or lack of strength to withstand physically demanding situation such as storms, floods and typhoons.

From a long term perspective and implications for gender relations, as women may end up spending more time on tasks that reinforce stereotypical gender roles. Thus, women are faced by a situation where their ability to adapt is low at the same time share of the adaptation burden falling disproportionately on them. This makes the consideration of the impact of climate change on gender most imperative.

The poor and marginalized segments in many societies which referes women, the elderly, immigrants, indigenous and groups of abject people. Those are particularly vulnerable to climate change impacts men and women differently, largely due to their gender-differentiated relative powers, roles and responsibilities because they are highly dependent on local natural resources for their livelihood. Women charged with securing water, food and fuel for cooking and heating face the greatest challenges. Women experience unequal access to resources and decision-making processes, with limited mobility in rural areas so as important to identify gender-sensitive strategies that respond to these crises for women[4].

The various factors have accounted for the discrepancy between women and men which differentiated exposure and vulnerability to climate changing risks. On the one hand, gender-based differences in time use, access to assets and credit and treatment by markets and formal institutions including the legal and regulatory framework constrain women's opportunities. As a result, there is a global gender gap in earnings and productivity women make between 30 to 80 percent of what men earn annually.

The World Bank survey in 141 countries have shown that 103 countries continue to impose legal differences on the basis of gender that may hinder women's economic opportunities[5]. In addition, two thirds of the worlds' 743 million illiterate adults are women.[6] The women have made up 43 percent of the overall agricultural labour force, percentages which varies by region and country. Overall, women make up half of the agricultural labour force in the least developing countries, they own between 10 to 20 percent of the land.[7] The cumulative effects of poverty and social, economic and political barriers of women often seem to be disadvantaged in coping with the adverse impacts of the changing climate.[8]

On the other hand, compared to men, women face huge challenges in accessing all levels of policy and decision-making processes. This renders them less able to influence policies, programmes and decisions which impact their lives. Further, socio-cultural norms limit women from acquiring the information and skills necessary to escape or avoid hazards.[9] Similarly, dress codes imposed on women that are restricted their mobility in times of disaster, as their responsibility for children to take care them. Eventually, lack of sex disaggregated data in all sectors often leads to an underestimation of women's power.

Gender equality for sustainable development

The global leaders have given voiced to continue their Summit on the Sustainable Development Goals, United Nations hosted a landmark event on gender equality and women empowerment particularly former Secretary-General Ban Ki-moon declared that new Global Goals could achieve by ensuring the equal rights to women in all sphere of field. In order to attain the goal of women empowerment concrete steps is required so as policies measures is scaling up in education, health care, access to land and energy. This integrated focus has been the most reaffirming idea that comprehensive and transformative approach is needed in order to address structural barriers to gender equality and lay a solid foundation for the future.

The key is to draw lessons learned from the experience of the Millennium Development Goals (MDGs) and strengthen the tools advanced gender equality in the desired areas. The major achievement of Millennium Development Goal of gender equality and development perspective has presented as follows

- Gender parity has been achieved in primary education however, only 2 of 130 countries have achieved this goal at all levels of education.
- Progress has been made in access to employment of women which is accounted 40 percent of paid jobs in sectors across in global which is mainly derived from agriculture and allied sectors
- The large spectrum (80%) of women are displaced by climate change
- The global gender gap in earnings and productivity persists across all forms of economic activity; women make between 30 to 80 percent of male annual income
- In developing countries, 10 to 20 percent of landholders are women
- Burning biomass fuel indoors leads to 2 million deaths per year which are women and children.
- In the developing countries, an annual average of more than 200 million people was affected and more than 70,000 people were killed by natural disasters particularly by water-related disasters.
- The average percentage of women members of parliament in the world was just over 22. 4 per cent. India is at 103 places of 140 countries with a 12 percent of representation[10].
- The MDGs have to address key issues such as violence against women, unpaid care work, women's control over assets and property, wage and sex discrimination, health and reproductive rights, and unequal participation in public and private decision-making at all levels. They also focus to make sufficient progress in the reduction of maternal mortality.

The challenges need to address as follows:

- **Comprehensive approach:** Set specific gender equality targets for each of the goals;

- **Implementation**: Transform the goals into public policies with sufficient resources to address inclusion and empowerment of women in all spheres;
- **Measurement and accountability**: Build a set of gender-related indicators that will allow us to assess the situation in real time and focus on what works[11].

Women and climate change

Women play a pivotal role in natural resources management, productive and reproductive activities. These activities have brought them in a position to contribute in livelihood strategies which are adapted to change environmental realities. Their extensive knowledge and expertise could utilize in climate change for mitigation, disaster reduction and adaptation strategies in order to effectively scale up the climatic changes and also they act as efficient climate change agents.

Consequently, women play a leadership role in early warning systems and reconstruction. Women tend to share information related to community well-being, choose less polluting energy sources and adapt more easily to environmental changes when their family's survival is at stake[12]. Women in South Asia displayed enormous strength and capacity throughout the entire disaster cycle such as preparing for hazards, managing after a disaster and rebuilding damaged livelihoods. Activities included ensuring food and water for the family, securing seed and other productive material and taking care of the sick and elderly.[13]

Plethora of research has revealed the importance of gender equality and women's empowerment to environmental sustainability and achievement of the Millennium Development Goals. The female participation in economic development leads to productivity gains. If women paid employment rates were raised to the same level as men, women tend to very effective at mobilizing communities in the event of disasters and disaster risk management and reduction and have a clear understanding of what strategies are needed at the local level.

With changes in climate, traditional food sources become more unpredictable and scarce which exposes women to loss of harvests, often their sole sources of food and income. Women are more dependent for their livelihood on natural resources that are threatened by climate change. The climate change causes a rise in the sea level, affecting the fishing community not only in terms of fish-catch but also with regard to water scarcity, as seawater gets into fresh water. Besides, when the land is inundated, infrastructure are damaged. Large scale migration from inundated areas is expected and much of the burden of migration falls on women. Climate change may exacerbate existing shortages of water. Women are taking responsible for water collection in their communities which affects when the quantity of water and accessibility changes. As primary caregivers, women responsibilities increase as family members suffer with illness due to exposure to vector borne diseases such as malaria and water borne diseases such as cholera and increase in heart stress mortality

Role of women as climate change agent

Gender equality is a fundamental human right however there are economic imperatives is needed for promotion of equality in climate development, community management, natural resource and biodiversity management, education of children and family care place them at the centre of development. They are the collectors of fuel and water for their families, and users of energy to prepare food and care for the sick which provides them in a position to contribute to livelihood strategies adapted to changing environmental conditions.

In general women are got more awareness and also adequate knowledge and capabilities to effectively scale up the climate change in order to mitigate, disaster reduction and adaption strategies. In developing countries, they engage substantially in agricultural production, both paid and unpaid. Thus, recognizing and supporting the activities and needs of women is essential for socio-economic development[14]. Participation of women enhances the effectiveness and sustainability of climate change projects and programmes are helped to address existing inequities while working towards fulfilling the respective international agreements calling for the equality and empowerment of women.

Conclusion

In the rapid climate changing world, women are most important resource to mitigate the climatic condition more feasible manner by leverage the changing trends of climate by utilizing their expertise with applying various methods and strategies such as saving waters and enabling the awareness on planting trees and also creating public assets. In order to control the climatic changes, the women need to recognize their activities in all the field and also get their rights for acting as a change agent. In the term of women empowerment and equality to scale up effectively the issues and challenges of both women and men and priorities, ensure the meaningful participation of women to attain the gender-equitable outcomes. So as climate change actions on consultation with women, build and incorporate their skills and knowledge, and provide opportunities for improving health, education and livelihoods. Increasing women's participation result in more environmental and productivity gains and create mutual benefits and greater returns across the Millennium Development Goals.

Gender considerations and women's issues, needs and contributions integrate across the planning and execution cycle of climate change policies and projects. There is a task to ensure mitigation and adaptation efforts also address sources of gender-based vulnerability, gender inequality and poverty because economic, legal and socio cultural constraints lead to women capacity gaps, climate change responses need to address women historic and current disadvantages. Legal and socio cultural barriers also inhibit women from responding on climate risk. In order to bring out the change in women equality ensures the women participation in environmental, social and economic development.

The women empowerment and gender equality is beneficial for family and community wellbeing and livelihoods are key factors in promoting the resiliency of economies and communities. The actions, technologies and strategies need to leverage the pro-poor and gender-responsive in their design, implementation, monitoring and evaluation and looking forward, the Nationally Appropriate Mitigation Actions and National Adaptation Plans established under the United Nations Framework Convention on Climate Change provide opportunities to develop climate change policy and implement projects that benefit women and contribute towards the broader effort of responding to the ill-effects of climate change.

The role of the government to incorporate gender perspectives into national and international climate chance finance mechanisms and strategies for efficient, effective and inclusive financing, gender must play an essential role, informing all policies and programming. In this effort, gender-sensitive structures, guidelines, projects and tools need to develop for all climate change financing mechanisms[15]. Supporting adaptation and mitigation actions, at all levels. In addition to that help to address the historical, political and socio-economic constraints faced by many women and sustainable development objectives, gender-based criteria develop for fund allocation, including project identification, design and performance objectives.

Notes

1. Fifty-second session of the Commission on the Status of Women, 25 February to 7 March 2008 (http://www. un.org/women watch/ daw/csw/52sess.htm).
2. Source: WHO (2011)a.http://www.who.int/gender/whatisgender/ en/index.html
3. UNFCCC 1992,, ACCESSED Aug17, 2015https://unfccc.int/files/ essential-background/back ground publications- htmlpdf/ application/pdf/conveng.pdf.
4. UNDP Human Development report 2014. Sustaining Human Progress: Reducing Vulnerabilities and Building Resilience (Newyork : UNDP,2014); World Bank, Turn Down the Heat: Climate Extremes, Regional Impacts, and the Case for Resilience.
5. World Bank, Women, Business and the Law 2011:Removing barriers to economic inclusion, Washington DC, 2011.
6. United nations Educational, Scientific and cultural organization Institute of Statics, Global Atlas of Gender equality in education, Paris, 2012.
7. FAO, 2011, NOTE 7: World Bank, World development Report 2012– Gender equality and development 2011.
8. Women Watch, 2009, Note : 7.
9. ROHR, U, ' Gender and Climate Change', TIEMPO, ISSUE 59, 2006: World Bank , Social Dimensions of climate change 2010.
10. the data on women in parliament from Lokshaba. Inter Parliamentary Union (data complied as of 1st January 2015)
11. via UN News Centre 27 Sep 2015 | Goal 5: Gender equality, News)
12. International Union for conservation of nature and Natural resources Gender aspects of climate change 2007)
13. via UN News Centre 27 Sep 2015 | Goal 5: Gender equality, News) Airya bandu M.M. the impact of Hazards on women and children available htpp://gdnonline, org/resources/airyabandu-paperdoc.)
14. United Nations Conference on Trade and Development, 'Applying a Gender Lens to Science, Technology and Innovation', Current Studies on Science, Technology and Innovation, 5th ed., Geneva, 2011)
15. Finance Mechanisms', UNDP, November 2010; UNDP, 'Ensuring Gender Equity in Climate Change Financing', 2011)

14

Role of Gram Sabha to Promote the Social Justice: A Case of Tamil Nadu

— Dr. A. Ranjithkumar and Dr. K. Barathiraja

Abstract

In the modern era provides opportunities to promote the social justice of women by participating in Grama Sabha. The Gram Sabha is the legislative body or mini legislature of rural local government and its responsibility for the preparation of plans in economic development and social justice. The recent result of local body elections is evidence that the participation women are increased. Hence, the rural areas recorded high percentage of polling (81.81 per cent) whereas in the urban areas the poll percentage recorded is marginally less (72.52 per cent). The study is an attempt to understand the role of Grama Sabha for enabling the process of economic development and social justice among the abject community at rural level.

Introduction

The Gram Panchayat has made possibilities to improve the facilities at village level such as drinking water, drainage, street light, road and transport, education and integrated women sanitary complex. In order to attain the welfare and development of village community particularly the women, the Village Panchayat has opened the enabling factor that Gram Sabha which provides the equality to women in the context of socio-economic and political welfare and development in participatory manner at planning of programmes, implementation, monitoring, evaluation and follow up (Palanithurai-2017).

Tamil Nadu has a long history of local government. The government of Madras Constituted a Committee in 1882 to study local administration. It recommended a three-tier system. A village or group of villages referred to as "union" formed the lowest tier; a Taluk forming a part of the revenue district formed the middle tier, the district constituted the top tier. The Royal Commission on Decentralization set up in 1906 gave its report in 1909, favouring the three-tier system. The commission also advocated that a substantial majority of the composition of members in local bodies should be elected. This was again reiterated by the Government of India Resolution in 1918. Further, the Montague-Chelmsford Reform also suggested that local 48 governments be placed under a native minister. The Madras Presidency then passed two parallel Acts taking into consideration the developments. (Nadu, 1999). These were:

- Madras Local Boards Act of 1920, and,
- Madras Village Panchayat Act of 1920.

Both provided for a three tier structure. Tamil Nadu, 1996 Tamil Nadu state has a three tier system, namely District Panchayat at the district level, Panchayat Union at the block level and Village Panchayat at the village level. Village Panchayat A Village Panchayat is constituted for a minimum of five hundred populations. A Village Panchayat would have members ranging from a minimum of five to a maximum of fifteen. The Ward Members and the President are to be elected directly by the voters. The Vice-President of the Village Panchayat is elected indirectly among the elected ward members of the Village Panchayat. All Village Panchayat will get their financial resources from the Government directly without any intermediary. The Panchayat Union or the Block Panchayat will not interfere in the process. The Gram Panchayat Presidents have been designated as Executive Heads and they have been entrusted with powers and responsibilities. There are 12,620 Village Panchayats in the State spread across the 30 districts and the 385 Blocks. The average number of Village Panchayats per district is 421 and per Block are 32. Now it has been incresead based on increasing number of district in Tamil Nadu. (Nadu, 1999)

Duties of Village Panchayats

Tamil Nadu Panchayats Act 1994, Section 110, constitutes the following as duties of village panchayat particularly the Grama Sabha. In these elections, over 2.45 lakhs ballot boxes were used in 60,514 polling stations in rural local bodies. And 78,903 EVMs were used in 25,877 polling stations in urban local bodies. Around 6.30 lakhs polling personnel were deployed.

- Building village panchayat roads and bridges and inscriptions on such roads, improvement and maintenance of them regularly.
- Set up street lights in residential areas, public roads, streets and public places and its maintenance.
- Ensure adequate availability of safe drinking water
- Implementation of appropriate projects directly or through the Panchayat Union or Drinking Water Board, Establishment of keyboards, pumps, public pumps, and providing housing at places where there is a possibility and maintaining such drinking water projects.
- Building public expenditure to improve public health in rural areas, establish health facilities in schools
- Helping people to provide shelter facilities in homes, thereby making the rural environmental pollution possible to prevent personal hygiene

- Prevention of environmental pollution in rural areas, especially water bodies prevention of pollution, disposal of waste water canals and removal of debris and waste from the streets
- Protect the trees and plant nutrients Shrubs, Bruises, Lungs, and Health Hazards that Hurt the Public Health and Safety
- Establishment and maintenance of graveyard and firearms
- Expanding villagers and organizing buildings
- Implementation of Mahatma Gandhi National Rural Employment Guarantee Scheme in the rural areas and the Central and State Government other projects

Optional Duties of Grama Sabha

In 1994, the Tamil Nadu Panchayats Act, Section 111, the following duties as per requirement and financial resources village panchayats carry out

- Planting trees on both sides of the road
- Set up and maintain street lights on roads along the areas of residential and buildings
- Set up and maintain public markets
- Provide health facilities in local festivals and markets
- Maintain the parking lot, bus stop, livestock stables
- Setting up the Meadows
- Maintain and maintain passenger lodging
- Prepare and maintain Radio, TV rooms, playgrounds and parks
- Set up and maintain fitness centers
- Conducting informal education, social education and adult education centers.

In order to ascertain the progressive of the Gram Panchayat goals and its programme the Grama Sabha plays a vital role in Development Team, Appointment team, Agriculture Committee, Work Committee and Education Committee

- **Appointment committee:** headed by Gram Panchayat leaders and members. The appoint committee plays a key role in the selection process of employees
- **Development Committee:** one of the female members of the village panchayat is the chairman of the committee and two members looking after the major development area such as health, drinking water and creating community assets.
- **Agriculture Committee:** the Chairman of this committee is one of the members of the Village Panchayat and enabling the use of modern technologies in irrigation sources, agricultural groups, agriculture, horticulture, dairy development, drought development, drought development, social forests, land management and soil erosion prevention.
- **Actions Committee:** local resource in village panchayat areas to fulfill the Central and State Government programs and developing plans using resources.
- **Education Committee:** monitoring of the activities of all schools in rural areas and infrastructure in schools and obtain people participation in promotion, adult education and library care.

Gram Sabha: A Glance

The Grama Sabha is the indicator for development of Gram Panchayat so as it is centered in order to provide welfare and development at villag level particualry women development. The feature of Gram Sabha

- The Gram Sabha is the foundation of the democratic system and control the panchayat administration

- Planning and implementation of rural local bodies
- Community Development

The Grama Sabha conducts in every Gram Panchayats on January 26, May 1, August 15, and October 2 for enabling the rural communities welfare and development.

Duties of Gram Sabha

- Approving the yearly development plan of village Panchayats.
- Recognize the list of beneficiaries for individual benefit programs and social assets Recognize the selected places for creation.
- Progress of projects like Indira Memorial Residential Plan, Mahatma Gandhi National Rural Employment Guarantee Scheme and Inspection of functions.
- Monitoring the quality of work done by Village Panchayats through Social and Technical Censorship.
- Evaluate Annual audit report and audits of the Village Panchayat
- Encourage social cohesion and religious harmony.
- Community, Census Board, Administration of Village Panchayats, Project Activities and Budgets Act as an audit system.

Key functions of Gram Sabha

- Help to implement the development programmes and schemes of the Panchayat.
- Beneficiaries identification for different programmes and schemes.
- Solicit support in cash or kind or both and voluntary labour from the public for community welfare programmes.
- Support the programmes of mass education and family welfare.

- Promote unity and harmony among all sections of the society in the village.
- Discuss and recommend appropriate action with regard to reports of the Vigilance. Committee and other related matters brought to the notice of the Gram Sabha.
- Fixing the levy of taxes, rates, rents and fees and enhancement of rates.

Social Mobilization, Social Justice and leadership of Women

Women have actively participated in People's movement in some parts of the country such as Chipko Movement in Uttarakhand, Narmada Bachao Andolan in Gujarat, Anti-liquor movement launched by women in Andhra Pradesh etc. and thus their leadership has emerged. Later, constitutional provision of one - third reservation for women in membership and leadership in Panchayat has widened the horizon of social mobilization of women in the country as a whole. This mobilization may be termed as peaceful revolution towards democracy and development. This is the achievement of gender equality in politics which is yet to merge in any democracy of the world. This dimension of social justice may be considered as a first step of social movement. The leadership of women in PRIs in some of the stated has been overshadowed presently by men. But in the process of political socialization their independent leadership may emerge in due course of time. It is unfortunate that active role of women in parliamentary politics is yet to be witnessed. Right from 1952 to 1996, it is evident from the results of all elections that not more than 9 percent of women members could be elected for parliament so far. Female population constitutes 48.1 percent of the total population and if they are kept away from the political activities, the society will not move towards development and social justice. Therefore, increase in their participation in PRIs in important dimension of political development as well as social development i the society. (Bishoyi, 2013).

Last local body elections of Tamil Nadu a total of 3.31 lakh voters, including 1.67 lakh women, and 2,277 transpersons, will cast their votes in the rural local elections. The rural areas recorded high percentage of polling (81.81 per cent) whereas in the urban areas the poll percentage recorded is marginally less (72.52 per cent). The overall poll percentage in the Local body election, 2011 is 78.80 which is higher than all the previous ordinary local body elections. Thouh this participation of women have been increased in this election. Moreover, women candidates also equally elected because of maintined their reservation. Now all level of the local elections obiviously the women candidates are more in the position of decision making. In this situation, the social needs which is mentioned above and welfare measures related expecting to favour of women.

Conclusion

The Grama Sabha is imperative for enabling the women welfare and development at villag level by providing basic amenities such as drinking water and women integrated sanitary complex. Without rolr and domination of men women can freely acting and involving all kind of decision making of Gram Pachanyat in Gam Sabha meeting perfunctorily enjoying their social justice. It is understood from the study that the Gram Sabha has opened up the livelihood opportunities through various activities particularly implementing employment based projects among village community for enhancing their socio-economic condition. Moreover, it is people centric approach whereas it provides equal opportunities to contribute in the development process of village so as Gram Sabha is considered as an extension mechanism for rural development especially for women welfare and development.

References

- Palanithurai, G. (2017): "Why is Gram Sabha important in our democracy?" https://www.youtube.com/watch?v=vdMJtGn1wbA, Uploaded on 08.04.2017, Accessed on 13.12.2018.
- N.C. Joshi (2008): 'Women Welfare – A Priority on the Government's Agenda', Kurukshetra, Vol. 56, No. II, pp. 7-9.
- G. Palanithurai (2001), Empowerment of Women: Problems faced by the elected Women Representatives—Experience from Tamil Nadu, Gandhigram: Rajiv Gandhi Chair for Panchayati Raj Studies, 49.
- Bandyopadhyay, D., & Mukherjee, Amitava (2004). New Issues in Panchayati Raj. New Delhi: Concept Publishing Co.
- Kaushik, Susheela (1993). Women and Panchayati Raj. New Delhi: Har-Anand publications.
- India Development Review (IDR) in Politics, Prime Ministerial, Can Gram Panchayats Ensure Rural Development And Social Justice Without Proper Training? https://www.youthkiawaaz.com/2019/12/strengthening-panchayats-in-india/ uploaded on 21.12.2019, accessed on 12.01.2020.
- Government of Tamil Nadu, Tamil Nadu Panchayats Act 1994, Chennai: Government of Tamil Nadu, 1994.
- Human Rights Advocacy and Research Foundation, Tamil Nadu Federation of Women Presidents of Panchayat Government, http://hrf.net.in/federation-of-women-panchayat-presidents/ accessed on 12.12.2019.

15

Causes of Girl Children Drop-out in Rural Areas – An Analysis

— M. Eswari

Introduction

The education is a basic need and right of every human being. It seeks to develop innate inner capacities of man. Education gives knowledge and develops a perspective of looking of prosperous life. In this context the present study has tried to find out the causes of girl children drop out in education at rural level. The dropout means leaving a school or group for practical reasons, necessities, or disillusionment with the system from which the individual in question leaves. The school dropouts are primary, upper primary students who do not maintain academic performance or cope with institutional requirements and ultimately leave the school without complete their education.

In addition to that early marriage is one of the major causes of girl child school dropout. The community value and widely practice early marriage which interrupts and denies girls education and prevents them to rise to their full potentials in order to participate in the development of their community. The economic factor is the other major cause for girl's school drop-out where most parents were not able to pay school fees due to abject poverty. Poverty is one of the leading causes of girl child school drop-out. Most Parents and Guardians are poor and cannot afford to provide food to their families due to financial constraints. Furthermore, the prevalence of civil unrest and insecurity in the country has destabilized learning in schools which has further caused school drop-outs. The school going children are at high risk of victimization, violence, abuse as they move long distances to their schools, this created fear in parents and forced them to restrict their girl children from going to school.

Major Factors to increase the girl children school dropout

- Girls begin working at an earlier age than boys especially in rural areas and girls also tend to do more work in the household than boys. In general, girls take more loads of household chores than the boys. On the other hand, rural girls do more household works than urban girls.
- Inadequate sanitation facilities in schools massively affect girls' dropout because this inadequacy indicates that schools are not safe for girls.
- School distance is considered too far from home, young girls tend to drop out more due to for the vulnerability to sexual harassment.
- Parents are afraid for the safety of their children when they have to travel longer distances to school.
- Rural areas girls' dropout rate became higher because parents consider girls' schooling as of no benefit when they leave their own family after getting married rural areas girls' dropout rate became higher because parents consider girls' schooling as of no benefit when they leave their own family after getting married.
- The traditional values and religious beliefs constrain girls from making their own decisions and expressing their own opinions

Scope of the study

The study has undertaken to examine the status and cause influencing girl child drop-out in Karur District.

Objectives

- To study the socio-economic status of the dropout girl children in rural areas
- To find out the causes of girl child school drop-out in rural areas
- To suggest ways and strategies to reduce girl child school drop-out.

Data collection tool and techniques

The researcher has used the Interview schedule for data collection and data analysed with simple percentage technique.

Limitations of the study

- The study is restricted with particular subjected to only the girl children.
- The study was limited with only in Karur district due to time and cost constraints.

The Major findings of the study

The study findings has discussed about the respondents age, marital status, occupation, reasons for dropout and strategies for mitigating the dropout ration among the girl children at grassroots level.

The researcher has presented the study result in the following tables and figures for understanding situation persisting to girl children which affects the education and their empowerment so as the appropriate strategies and concrete steps have to take by the Government in order to provide welfare and development measures to the girls children which enables the knowledge, skills and empowerment.

Table 15.1: Distribution of the Respondents by Age.

Sl. No.	*Age*	*No. ofrespondents*	*Percentage*
1.	11-14	5	10
2.	15-18	8	16
3.	19-22	22	44
4.	23 above	15	30
	Total	**50**	**100**

The table 15.1 indicates that, 10 percent of the respondents belonged to 11-14 years, followed by 16 percent of the respondents belonged to 15-18 years, 44 percent of the respondents belonged to 19-22 years and 30 percent belonged to above 23. The study may be implied that the majority of the women under the age group of 19-22 years so as the education is vital to them for enabling their career.

Table 15.2: Distribution of the Respondents by Marital Status.

Sl. No.	*Marital status*	*Number of Respondents*	*Percentage*
1.	Married	37	74
2.	Unmarried	13	26
	Total	**50**	**100.0**

The table 15.2 shows that a large spectrum (74%) of the respondents is married, followed by (26%) are unmarried. The study may be confined that the girl children are married in their young age which has led them to discontinue and drop out from the schooling.

Table 15.3: Distribution of the respondents by occupation.

Sl. No.	*Occupation*	*Number of Respondents*	*Percentage*
1.	Coolie	27	54
2.	Private	04	08
3.	Government	01	02
4.	Self Employment	04	08
5.	Not Applicable	14	28
	Total	**50**	**100**

The table 15.3 indicates that occupation of the respondents, 54 percent are coolies, 8 percent of the respondents were working in private companies, 2 percent of the respondents were government employees and 8 percent were self employees. 28 percent of the respondents were unmarried. The study may be concluded that the most of the women are working as coolie after dropping out from the schooling.

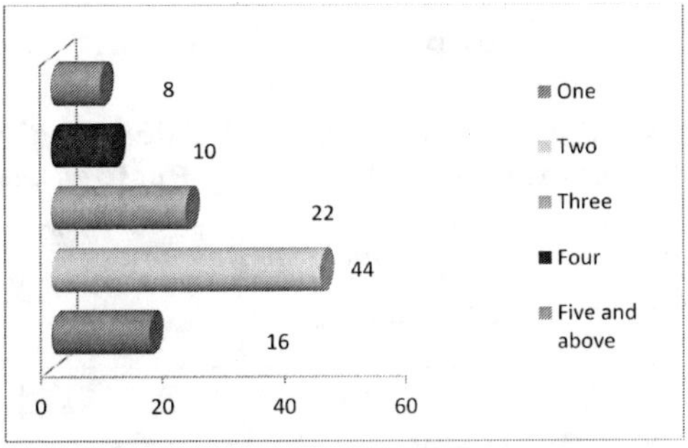

Figure 15.1: Distribution of the Respondents by Number of Siblings.

The figure 15.1 shows that, 16 percent of the respondents have one sibling, 44 percent have 2 siblings, 22 percent have three siblings, 10 percent have 4 siblings and 8 percent have more than 5 siblings. Girl children take care of their siblings in rural areas. The study may be confined that girl children have a significant level of siblings which has led them to forward as well as backward to school and de-schooling.

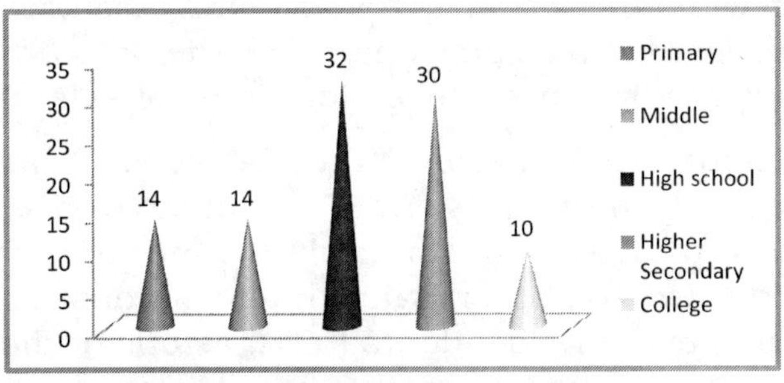

Figure 15.2: Distribution of the Respondents by Dropout from School.

The figure 15.2 shows that, respondents drop out. Each 14 percent of the respondents were dropout their primary education and middle school level. 32 percent of the respondents were dropout high school level. 30 percent of the respondents were dropout their higher secondary level, 10 percent of the respondents were dropout college level. The study is evident that the girl children has dropped out from schooling when they studied the high and higher secondary school at large level which may be caused due to the family circumstances.

Table 15.4: Distribution of the Respondents by Distance of School from Residence.

S.No	*Distance of School*	*Number of Respondents*	*Percentage*
1.	1-2 km	6	12
2.	3-4 km	14	28
3.	5-6 km	15	30
4.	7-8 km	08	16
5.	9km and above	07	14
	Total	**50**	**100.0**

The table 15.4 indicates the distance between school and residence, 32.5 percent said that they have to go for 2 KM from residence. 24.6 percent said the school is located in 1 KM distance, 15.8 percent mentioned that the school is located within 0.5 KM, 14 percent have to go for 3 KM and 13.2 percent have to go for above 4 KM from residence to school. The study may be implied that the distance of schooling determines the dropout rate of girl children when the school is located nearby their area there is less dropout at the same time when the school distance increases the dropout rate is increased considerably.

The figure 15.3 indicates that, 34 respondents (68%) said that early marriage is one of the causes of girls school dropped-out. This is particularly a hindrance to girl's education. On the other hand financial constraint was mentioned by 31 respondents (62%) as one of the major causes of girls school drop-out. These indicate that due to financial problem most parents cannot afford to pay

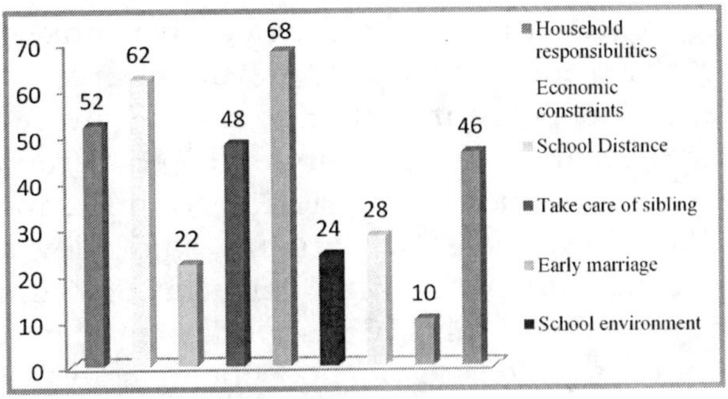

Figur 15.3: Distribution of the Respondents by Causes of girls children drop-out.

their children school fees. 26 respondents (52%) said that take care of household responsibilities is one of the causes of girls school dropped-out. Not interest in studies said by 14 respondents (28%). 24 percent of the respondents said school environment like inadequate facilities in the school, 22 percent of the respondents said school distance go far from the residence. 10 percent of the respondents felt that illness and death of parents is causes of dropout and 46 percent of the respondents said that traditional

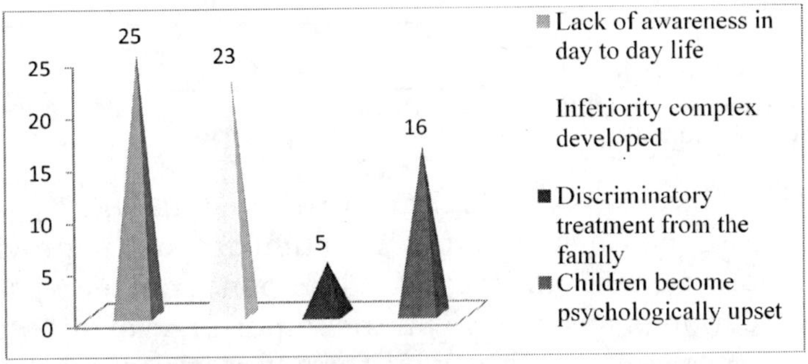

Figure 15.4: Distribution of the Respondents by Consequences of being a Dropout.

beliefs that it's a waste of resource. The study may be concluded that the family circumstances and their financial abject condition have led the girl children to discontinue their education and made decision to do marriage and taking family responsibilities.

The figures 15.4 indicates the negative consequences faced by the respondents of being a drop out, 25 respondents (50 percent) felt that lack of awareness in day to day activities, 23 respondents (46 percent) said that the development of inferiority complex in public places, 5 respondents (10 percent) said they are not enjoying social status and they felt that discriminatory treatment from the family. 16 respondents (32 percent) of the respondents child's become psychologically upset due to my parents were illiterate. The study may be confined that the dropout of girl children is led them to lack of awareness, complexity, low confidence and physical and psychological disorder.

Table 15.5: Distribution of the Respondents by ways and strategies to reduce girl child drop-out.

Ways and strategies to reduce dropout	*Number of Respondents*	*Percentage*
Provide free boarding schools for girls	41	82
Create awareness about importance of girls education	24	48
Provide free transport facilities for girl students	43	86
Create awareness about causes of early marriage	33	66
Provide sanitary napkin changing room in all school and college	29	58

The table 15.5 reveals that 41 respondents (82%) said that one of the ways to reduce girl child dropout to provide free boarding schools for girls. 24 respondents (48%) said that creation of awareness on the importance of girl child education is yet another way to reduce girl child drop-out. 43 respondents (86%) said that to provide free transport facilities for girls children. 33 respondents (66%) said that to create awareness about causes of early marriage and 29 respondents (58%) said that to provide sanitary napkin changing room in all school and college.

The study may be implied that the appropriate strategies is needed to scale up the girl children education and mitigating the dropout rates at village level so that the free education, food and quality education lead them to continue their education. Moreover, the education is the key element for their career development so as they want to grab their educational rights from their family and Government.

Findings

- Major findings of the study, Majority (44 percent) of the respondents belonged to 19-22 years and 30 percent belonged to above 23. 32 percent of the respondents were dropout high school level.
- 30 percent of the respondents were dropout their higher secondary level, only 10 percent of the respondents were dropout college level.
- Majorities (74 percent) of the respondents were married and 26 percent are married. Most (54 percent) of the respondents, 22 percent of the respondents have one sibling, 18 percent have 2 siblings, 22 percent have three sibling, 10 percent have 4 siblings and 8 percent have more than 5 siblings. So, Girl children were taking care of their siblings in rural areas.
- 32.5 percent said that they have to go for 2 KM the distance between school and residence and 13.2 percent have to go for above 4 KM from residence to school.
- Majority of the (68 percent) respondents said that early marriage is one of the causes of girls school dropped-out.
- This is particularly a hindrance to girl's education. On the other hand financial constraint was mentioned by 62 percent of the respondents as one of the major causes of girls school drop-out. These indicate that due to financial problem most parents cannot afford to pay their children school fees.

- 52 percent of the respondents said that take care of household responsibilities is one of the causes of girls school dropped-out. 24 percent of the respondents said school environment like inadequate facilities in the school, 22 percent of the respondents said school distance go far from the residence. 10 percent of the respondents felt that illness and death of parents is causes of dropout and 46 percent of the respondents said that traditional beliefs that it's a waste of resource.
- 50 percent felt that lack of awareness in day to day activities, 46 percent said that the development of inferiority complex in public places, 10 percent said they are not enjoying social status and they felt discriminatory treatment from the family. 32 percent of the respondents children's become psychologically upset due to my parents were illiterate.
- Majority (81 percent) of the respondents said that one of the ways to reduce girl child dropout to provide free boarding schools for girls. 48 percent of respondents said that creation of awareness on the importance of girl child education is yet another way to reduce girl child drop-out. Most of the respondents (86 percent) said that to provide free transport facilities for girls children.
- 66 percent respondents said that to create awareness about causes of early marriage and 29 respondents (58 percent) said that to provide sanitary napkin changing room in all school and college. Most of the (31 percent) respondents felt they are not able to continue education due to their economic condition and crossing certain age limit.

Conclusion

The education is the key enabling factor for welfare and development of the girl children which enables their rights and provides livelihood opportunities. Moreover, education bridges the gap between the gender disparities. In order to ensure the girl education, the Government has made up appropriate policies and Acts for enabling their educational career and employment opportunities at priority basis and provides advocacy, free educational kit and special education. Further, Government provides adequate awareness to increase the girl schooling rate significant level sensitizing the community on the importance of girl child education and providing scholarship and educational loan retain the girl children in schooling and higher studies for sustainable educational career development and welfare.

Reference

1. Cardoso & Vernon (2007). Cited in Srivastava, P. (2012) Psychosocial factors of dropout students in elementary and Middle schools. Rajeev Gandhi Shiksha Mission Project. SoS in Psychology, Pt. Ravishankar Shukla University, Raipur
2. Chanakira, E. (1986) "Primary schools dropouts". In: Chivore, B.R. S. (1985) Educational administration and management. Harare: Ministry of Higher Education.
3. Chivore, B.R.S. (1985) Educational administration and management. Harare: Mazongororo Paper Converters (Pvt) Ltd.
4. Chugh, S. (2011) Dropout in Secondary Education: A study of children living in slums of Delhi, Occasional Paper No. 37, NUEPA, New Delhi.
5. IIE (Indian Institute of Education) (2006) A study of the extent and causes of dropouts in primary schools in rural Maharashtra with special reference to girl dropouts, Pune
6. Kasente D. (2003). Gender and Education in Uganda: A Case Study for Monitoring Report, Makerere University

16

An analysis of women empowerment in various fields in India

— Mr. Nagappa L H

Abstract

The women empowerment has become the major issues across the world. Since last few decades women empowerment is a debatable subject at earlier time they were getting equal status with men in Vedic period. But they have faced in some difficulties during earlier period to since medieval in modern society many times they were treated as slave. But 21th century their status has been changed slowly and gradually in society in women status. The Indian constitution gave the equal, liberal, political, social, economic, cultural, education, and other rights have given to women. They are natural born social leaders so as occupied the respectable positions in various fields such as Political, Social, Educational, Industrial entrepreneur and great leaders. At the same time, women are not absolutely free in the society because gender discrimination, caste, class, sexual harassment, society hierarchy, and pay scale discrimination. In order to improve their livelihood opportunities and welfare development the fellow people and all the men people have to support to protect and promote from the social evils and also enable their freedom at work place as well as at home in particularly user-friendly manner.

Key word: *women empowerment, 21th century woman's condition, constitution, social hierarchy, women problems, and emerging their life, women empowerment schemes etc.*

Introduction

Women empowerment refers to increasing the spiritual, political, social, education, and economic strength of individual and communities of women. Women empowerment in India is heavily dependent on many different variable that include geographical location urban and rural, educational, social status, caste and class. The principle of gender equality in enshrined in Indian constitution in its preamble fundamental rights, fundamental duties and directive principle. The constitution not only great equality women but also empower state to adopts measure of positive discrimination in favor of women with the framework of democratic polity or laws development policies plans and programs have aim at women's advancement in different sphere. In recent years the empowerment of women has been unorganized has central issues. In determining the status of women on attempt to analysis the status of women empowerment in India is using various indicators like women's household, decision making power, financial participation acceptance of unequal gender role exposure to media women achievement towards the goal. However depends largely on the attitude of the people towards gender equability women empower is also defined has a change in the context women life which enable her increase capacity for leading fulfilling human life it gets reflected both in external qualities health, mobility, education and awareness, status in the family participation in decision making and also at the level of material security and internal qualities self awareness and self confidence.

Objectives of the study

1. To know the need of women empowerment
2. To study the govt. sachem for women empowerment
3. To analysis the factors influencing the political empowerment

4. Be aware of the law and polices for women empowerment
5. To know the women empowerment issues
6. Making awareness about women's political rights and responsibilities

Need for women Empowerment

We can tell the condition of country by looking at the status of its women "said Neharu empowerment of women has become the solution to many societal problems. Rameshwari Pandy (2008) in 21 century women have to come out of their long cherished male supremacy and her weakness women must have capacity to battle issues of this global. Therefore women are worshiped goddess in India, but not given terms position the main problems facing by women in past and present. gender discrimination female infanticide, feticide , dowry early child marriage atrocities on women's with their age they have been raped killed sex stereotype domestic violence, women trafficking, honour killing, Eve teasing, sexual harassment at work place .

The national record bureau was conducted by crime against women at 5.4% sexual harassment dose not reflected a term picture , molestation 19%, cruelty by relatives and husband 43.9% , rape 10.5%, kidnapping abuduction12%, sexual harassment 5.4%, dowry deaths 4.1% , Dowry prohibition 2.8%, immoral trafficking 1.2%.

Women Empowerment in 21th century

Empowerment is a multi-dimensional process which should enable individuals or a group of individuals to realize their full identity and powers in all spheres of life. According to Webster's dictionary the word empowerment indicates the situation of authority or to be authorized or to be powerful. Empowerment is a process that gives a person freedom in decision making. The 21th century the term empowerment of women has become a well know subject on many occasions. The vast majority of the politicians so called well wishes of the public never left opportunity to talk about their concern and responsibility in giving priority to empowerment of women.

Education and Empowerment

Education as means of empowerment of women can bring about a positive attitude change, it therefore crucial for social economic and political entrepreneur progress of Indian constitution of India empower the state to adopt affirmative measures for promoting way and means empower women education significantly make difference in lives of women these can be direct or indirect being mentioned.

Improve the economic growth

Education increase the economic, social and political opportunities available to women it leaders direct economic beautiful in the form of higher life time earning for women. The society and country also benefits higher from the higher productivity of its labour force besides improving human capital an increasing economic growth female education. Also reduce the fertility rate. The lowering in the number of depends is referred to as the demographic gift.

Political Participation

At the grassroots levels 50% reservation given to women local self government insinuation as improved political participation of women in India, yet political participation of legislatives Assemble and parliament is still quite low in India women have abandoned the position of presidents prime minister speaker and cabinet ministers and political of opposition in politics of India and have proved their worth.

Year wise membership of women in the parliament

Years	*Members of Lokasabha*			*Years*	*Members of Rajasabha*		
	Total members	*Female*	*%*		*Total member*	*Female*	*%*
1951	499	22	4.41	1951	219	16	7.31
1957	500	27	5.40	1957	237	18	7.59
1962	503	34	6.76	1962	238	18	7.56
1967	521	31	5.93	1967	240	20	8.33
1971	523	22	4.22	1971	243	17	7.00
1977	544	19	3.49	1977	244	25	10.25
1980	544	28	5.15	1980	244	24	9.84
1984	544	44	8.09	1984	244	24	11.48
1989	517	27	5.22	1989	245	24	9.80
1991	554	39	7.17	1991	245	38	15.51
1996	543	39	7.18	1996	223	19	8.52
1998	543	43	7.92	1998	245	15	6.12
1999	543	49	9.0	1999	245	19	7.12
2004	539	44	8.2	2004	245	28	11.4
2009	543	58	10.6	2009	245	22	8.98
2014	543	61	11.2	2014	245	29	11.8

Source: Election commission of India.

The table depict on women participated in Indian parliament, in 1951 lokasbha only 22, (4.41) members and also rajsabha members 16, (7.31) but 2014 (16th) loksabha women members 61, (11.2%) and rajasbha members 29, (11.8%) . the women step by step increase to political participation that president, prime minster, cabinet minister, governors like others women's are successful participation political sector.

Women Empowerment Schemes

1. Beti Bachao Beti Padhao Scheme
2. One Stop Centre Scheme
3. Women Helpline Scheme
4. UJJAWALA: A Comprehensive Scheme for Prevention of trafficking and Rescue, Rehabilitation and Re-integration of Victims of Trafficking and Commercial Sexual Exploitation
5. Working Women Hostel

6. Ministry approves new projects under Ujjawala Scheme and continues existing projects
7. SWADHAR Greh (A Scheme for Women in Difficult Circumstances)
8. Support to Training and Employment Programmed for Women (STEP)
9. NARI SHAKTI PURASKAR
10. Awardees of Stree Shakti Puruskar, 2014 & Awardees of Nari Shakti Puruskar
11. Awardees of Rajya Mahila Samman & Zila Mahila Samman
12. NIRBHAYA
13. Mahila police Volunteers
14. Mahila E-Haat
15. Mahila Shakti Kendras (MSK)

Research methodology

Collecting information on Women Empowerment analysis has been drawn up through secondary sources Library, Books, Journals, Articles, Published books, research reports and Online sources.

Conclusion

India is progressive to become world's fastest growing economy in near future it must also focus on women empowerment we must understand that women empowerment is process which hopes to bring gender equality and balanced economy. Indian women had been President Prime minister, Civil service, Doctors, entrepreneur, Lawyers etc. But still good majority of them needs help and support. Support own to be educated to do what they want to do, to travel safe to work, safe and to be independent making their own decision the way to the socio-economic development of here women folk. Therefore women empowerment can be said to be the country way to development therefore every one need to work hand for women's empowerment in the present scenario.

Work cited

1. Ram sharam S. (1996) Education of Women Empowerment (2 volumes) New Delhi: Gyan Publishing house.
2. Sganda Lal (2011) Women Empowerment, Kunal Book Publisher.
3. Gill Rajesh, (2006) Empowering women through panchayats-stories of success and struggle from India.
4. Mazumdar, Vina (1979) Symbols of powers studies on the political status of women in India, Allied New Delhi.
5. Kumar (2006) Women Empowerment and Social Change, Anmol Publication Pvt. Lld, New Delhi.
6. Online sources

17

Overviews on Women Migration and Gender Issues

— *Mr. Vishwanath M Ainapur*

Abstract

Migration is the movement by people from one place another place with the intentions of settling, permanently or temporarily in a new location these movements is often over long distances and from one country to another country after 2nd world war number of migrater migrate to various country for jobs, higher education, marriage, slaves etc. Gender refers to the differences and communality between women and men. Which are set by convention and other social, economic, political, and cultural forces women's facing number of problems gender discrimination, sex segregated, labour market. Over the past few years next generation network migration has been one of the most popular to aspect in the world.

***Key words**: gender, migration, women problems, women problems etc.*

Introduction

Over the past 60 years female migrants have been almost as numerous as male migrants. In 1960 there were 35 million female migrants and 40 million male migrants; in 2000 the gap between females and males remained about the same 85 million female migrants versus 90 million male migrants. In the 1960s and early 1970s the phrase "migrants and their families" was a code for "male migrants and their wives and children." The women's movement, however, with its emphasis on the situation of women, caused some to question the near-invisibility of women as migrants, their presumed passivity in the migration process, and their assumed place in the home. The feminist view of gender as a "social construction" has raised two questions that have fuelled much of the research in the study of women and migration over the last decade.

The first relates to patriarchy, or the hierarchies of power, domination, and control men use to rule women. To promote labour exports, Asian governments have played a very active role. Female labour migration is a demand-driven, rather than a supply-driven, phenomenon. The volume and type of demand for migrant workers is determined within the context of the international and sexual division of labour. To respond to demand patterns in the host countries, labour-exporting countries have to promote female, and not just male, overseas contract work. In fact, demand from labour-importing countries for women migrants is often more stable than that for men, so that women migrants often represent a more reliable source of foreign exchange remittances than men. But sending countries have come under increasing pressure to protect their women migrants.

Today, despite shortcomings in statistics and varying definitions of a "migrant", it is known that at least 50 million women are international migrants, some 30 million of them in developing countries. In 1990, according to United Nations estimates, Asia was host to some 20 million female migrants, followed by North America and Europe with about 12 million each and Africa with over 7 million. Their participation in migration flows fluctuates over time and, because of differences in migration policies, varies from one receiving country to another. Women's migration is also shaped by their role in the country of origin. The growing attention paid to migrant women at the international level is an expression of the increasing focus on women's rights and special needs that has taken place over the last two decades in various fields. A number of studies during that time have led to specific recommendations and policies aimed at improving the survival and development of female children.

Women migration problems

1. Female migrant face major risks, including sexual exploitation, trafficking and violence.
2. Migrant women face double discrimination as women and as migrants.
3. Women do not stop getting pregnant when they are on the move.
4. She has face gender, class, caste, and cost, problems.
5. Migration women's face tradition, customs, cultural, and languages etc.

Immigration and emigration policies that enable women as well as men to take up opportunities that safe and regular migration may offer and which will foster the positive impacts of migration for the social and economic development of migrants and the receiving and sending countries.

Gender issues

Gender issues include all aspects and concerns related to women's and men's lives and situation in society, to the way they interrelate, their differences in access to and use of resources, their activities and how they react to changes, interventions and policies. In 2016, India ranked 130 out of 146 in the Gender Inequality Index released by the UNDP. It is evident that a stronger turn in political discourse is required, taking into consideration both public and private spaces. Gender inequality extends across various facets of society. Political participation is often perceived as a key factor to rectify this situation.

Major gender issues

1. Sex stereotype
2. Gender based discriminations
3. Gender inequalities
4. The status of Indian women
5. Domestic of women violence etc.

The gender issues depicted here are not only the review of literatures but also the result of observation of gender based issues in real situations and continuing effort for better ways of addressing it at the grassroots level. The word gender describes the socially constructed roles and responsibilities that societies consider appropriate for men and women. Gender equality means that men and women have equal power and equal opportunities for financial, independence, education, and personal development. Women empowerment is a critical aspect of achieving gender equality. It includes increasing woman's sense of self worth, her decision making power, her access to opportunities and resources, her power and control over her own life inside and outside the home and her ability to change.

Suggestions

1. Increase financial and human resources in migration prone areas.
2. Promote public- private partnership for promotion of safe internal migration.
3. The governments providing to all specialties for women development.
4. Avoid the gender based society.
5. The government should not discriminate against to women migrate etc.

Conclusion

One important facet of study on population is the study of migration arising out of various social, economic or political reasons. Thus migration as a component of population change has significance well beyond its impact on the changing population size and composition of a human settlement. In the paper depicts the women's migration and gender issues in present day, Gender issues is one of the most barriers in the society. But women's are increasing their rights. Now governments providing the all specialties but it's not reach to women improvements. At the national level, rather than addressing the causes of gender discrimination or the risks female migrants face, some governments have banned female migration as a means to protect women and children – a measure that contravenes women's human rights. Gender also shapes the migration experience, regardless of whether migration is voluntary or forced (see Box 1). Female migrants, particularly girls, have less information, less education, and fewer options for regular migration, which puts them at greater risk of exploitation and abuse, including trafficking (UNFPA, 2015). Farah (2006) reported that 80% of trafficking victims were estimated to be female. Girls migrating alone are particularly vulnerable (Temin et al., 2013). Female migrants tend to be more averse to risk than men, however, and prefer to migrate through regular channels and when social networks are in place (Fleury, 2016). Migrants often establish networks for social support; this enables other women and girls from their community to follow (Temin et al., 2013) and reduces the stigma caused by breaking traditional gender norms Finally I conclude that women migration and gender issues is one of problem, but 21th century improving the women empowerment and also women's show the their status in the world.

Works cited

1. Siddiqui. T (2001), Transcending Boundaries: Labour Migration of Women from Bangladesh, The University Press Limited.
2. Kaul. K (2006) Migration and socity, Rawat Publication, New Delhi.
3. Jayaram. N. Ed & intro. "Introduction: The study of Indian Diaspora". The Indian Diaspora: Dynamics of Migration. New Delhi: Sage Publications, 2004.

4. John. E Mary (2008) Women studies' in India, Penguin publication.
5. Menon. Nivedita (2001) Gender and Politics in India, Publisher OUP India.
6. Online sources

18

Role of Education in Empowerment of Rural Women

— *K. Pushpam, R. Subburaman*

Abstract

In the contemporary society, education is a key enable factor to women empowerment so as it has always looked upon education is vital element for welfare and development. In this context, entry of women into the formal system began in the mid 19th century by the social reformist, but it got wider acceptance only in the mid 20th century. These centuries has social reformation and national movements questioning the equal status and inferior feelings on women in the society. In this background, the present study describes the education is an instrument of social change which provides empowerment to the educated women in the family particularly at rural level.

Introduction

The economic empowerment is essential for women in raising their socio-economic condition status in the society. However, they are persisted the acute male-female disparity which curbs their rights and livelihood opportunities and socio-economic empowerment of women is directly linked with education. It is observed that even after decades of independence women have not been able to combat illiteracy so as which ultimately lead the women into poverty. The women, mostly has drawn from the rural background whereas they needed to shoulder up by earning money at abject income to support their family.

In order to improve their socio-economic condition education is the key elements particularly at grassroots level. The Social empowerment through education is the need of the hour to overcome all the poverties and social evils of women in all sphere of welfare and development.

The most important characteristics of women empowerment is termed as literacy which is pre-requisite for overall development of the country both socially and economically. It is a more sensitive index of social development compared to overall literacy rate. The female literacy is negatively related with fertility rates, population growth rates and infant and child mortality rates which show a positive association with female age at marriage, life expectancy and participation in modern economy.

In spite of all special constitutional provisions and governmental efforts in the field of education to ameliorate equalities among women and men due to the attitudinal changes of rural people they are believed that education is imperative for changing the life style pattern along with self-confidence, dignity and self determination capacity of the women to eliminate the implicit and explicit socio-economic disadvantages and disparities.

Statement of the problem

Women are most oppressed and neglected group in society at grassroots level. In tradition, women are considered as weaker section so they are given a subordinate status in Hindu society. Subsequently this has led to abuse and harassment of women even within the family. In India, violence at home is common in poor and illiterate families as often presumed. Women issues are transformed into societal issues. Consequently, Government has taken up so many reform policies to enable the women education across the country for providing livelihood opportunities to the women empowerment.

Review of the study

Bijayalaxmi Praharaj (2010) study conducted on "status In India and empowering them through education". The author has pointed out that In India, women and girls received far less education that men, due to both social norms and fear of violence, the country has the largest population of non-school going working girls. Indian constitution guarantees free primary school education for both boys and girls up to the age of 14. But it is not universal in India. Overall the literacy rate for women is 54.16 percent and 75.85 percent for men according to the census report of 2001. Despite the impressive increase in literacy rates during the 1990s, the backlog of non-literate people remains high in 2001, close to 296 million people were classified as non- literates out of which, 190 million are women.

Further, he has argued that illiterates do not have scientific attitudes of mind and out of ignorance; they suffer from blind beliefs, superstitious and other social taboos. They are also not health conscious; they have no requisite ideas of their rights and duties. Besides illiterates develop an inferiority complex and insecurity in them and self- esteem is not properly cultivated due to lack of education and they are not able to put forth their grievances for redress before the appropriate authorities.

It is also observed that they are not able to keep place with the rapid changes in the world due to knowledge explosion and not aware of different plans and programmes of development works undertaken in the country for their development. Illiteracy is a handicap for successful functioning of democracy in the country. A universal truth is that failure of democracy and poor functioning of democratic system and economic backwardness of the people are due to large scale illiterates. It is unfortunate that even after five decades of Independence we are not been able to combat illiteracy which ultimately leads to poverty.

Illiteracy low level of skills, lack of access to training and credit facilities, coupled with lack of entrepreneurship, invisible contribution to family economy and restricted mobility as a result of gender bias are some of the contributing factors for women subordination. Knowledge input is the main tool for women to come out of poverty but poverty a vicious multi-pronged evil has its significant adverse impact upon girls' education. The impact of education is seen in the life style and the size of the family. Generally educated working parents prefer single family, willing to enjoy greater freedom of association and movement. Educated girls exposed to wider world are changing their view as regards to marriage and life style. The effect of modernization has been evidenced in families also. The study found that the educated girls are married at a nature stage and prefer to select their spouses as their own interest.

Objectives of the study

- To study the socio-economic conditions of the rural educated women
- To identify the role of educated rural women to empower
- To find out the problems of the educated rural women
- To offer the remedial measures to issues and challenges of women empowerment

Operationalization of the study

Rural Educated Women: those who are coming under the educated women from the rural areas are called rural educated women.

Empowerment: empowerment has itself as a part of radical action which used freely and indiscriminately and capable of innumerable interpretations depending on who you are and your place in the complex of socio economic spheres.

Sources of Data

For the study, the researchers have used both primary and secondary data in order to scale up the objectives of the study.

Tools of Data Collection

The Researchers have used observation and focused group discussion techniques as tools for data collection.

The Major Findings of the Study

General Observation of women in Rural Area

- The study found during the field level observation that socio-cultural and educational status of Indian women began to change and slowly moved towards their upliftment and empowerment in the present society.
- The observed that literacy rate of India has increased due to national literacy Mission, it's a typically low level in rural areas is the hard truth which is caused due to poverty, gender bias, social attitude and lack of awareness.
- The study indicated that empowerment is a feasible solution for empowering women as education offers multifaceted benefits it is high time that India rushes to "sign up" in the two word mantras educate Girls" and invests in women and girls to harvest its manifold impacts.
- The study corroborated that education increases their skill and decision making
- The study found that Government has made possibilities to have education based on higher and technical quality to empower women for their welfare and development
- The study implied that education of women is of paramount importance for the development of individuality and act as an instrument for

strengthening socially useful skills, habits and attitudes of common citizenship.

- The study found that education is an essential factor in achieving economic development and technical progress and in creating social order founded on the values of freedom, social justice and equality of opportunities, to avoid social evils and taboos through educating them. Education of rural women also assumes great importance to enable them to get the fullest benefit of globalization.

Role of Educated women in the family

- The study observed that women play multiple roles such as mother, wife and daughter.
- The study found that Empowered Educated Rural Women (EERW) has convinced their family and also made arrangement to share their family responsibilities with family members such as mother in law.
- The study revealed that many of Empowered Educated Rural Women are willing to go for employment to get empowerment in financial and socio-economic freedom
- The study found that educated women have earning capacity by doing small business such as tailoring, sale of dress and small enterprises.
- The study found that educated women take tuition to local students to spend their time valuably and also earn little money to contribute their family financial strength.
- The study observed that educated women like to have political power whereas they competitive in local elections
- The study found that educated women are actively participated in social welfare activities such as Self-Help Group

Problems

- The study found that women are facing various problems and challenges such as gender bias, sexual harassments, limited freedom, less decision making power, low wages in working field and non-recognization for their achievements
- The study found that even the educated women are now allowed to work which disabled their potentiality
- The study revealed that girl child are not allowed to even sit in front of the male in many cases and forced to do household works and now willing to go for education

Remedial Measures

- The study found that education is the key change agent to women empowerment moreover which creates health environment, eradicate discrimination and protect from social evils.
- The study revealed that education builds the confidence, skills and decision making power to women
- The study found that education liberates women from ignorance and enhances their self-esteem and provides possible solution to their livelihood opportunities to enhance welfare and development at grassroots level.

Conclusion

The education is the key enable of women to have empowerment in all sphere of development particularly socio-economic empowerment. Moreover, it builds the inner confidence to meet out the social issues against them and enhancing their quality in order to enable their voice at family and society. The education provides opportunities to learn the employability skills to start their own business and strengthen their financial position to leverage their family socio-economic stability thereby get respected in family as well as society and which motivates them to participate in social welfare activities such as Self-Help Group and political administration to paradigm shift towards sustainable livelihood development and create integrated welfare among all section of people development at grassroots level.

References

- Bijayalaxmi Praharaj (2010), women's status in India and Empowering then through education, Abhijeet publications-Delhi-110094, ISBN: 978-93-80031-43-9
- krishna Bhonik (2006), Indian women the ushering of a New dawn, Mital Publication, New Delhi, ISBN: 81-8324-079-8
- susheela kaushik (1985), women's oppression patterns and perspectives, women in society, vikas publishing house, pvt, ltd. ISBN

19

Legalizing Prostitution: The Flip Side of a Coin

— Anagha Nair, Niranjana J Anil

Abstract

One of the coarsest creations of the patriarchal world that we find our abode in, is the institution of prostitution. Therein, the unrestrainable carnality and other sexual desires of men are to be quenched by the women subject to prostitution. Since, forever this practice of prostitution has existed and has blend like oxygen and water into the cultural history of India. Through this paper we aim to examine the presence of this institution in the history along with the present legal aspects of the same with definitions and dimensions of the same under practice in India. We will further discuss the special laws that have been enacted under the IPC for preventing prostitution in the territory of the country. Currently there is no legal status quo of prostitution in India. In the near past, the apex court recommended that the times have now changed and so should the rules, hence the government should look into the matters concerning prostitution and revise the legislations dealing the same. Via this paper we also intend to discuss the burning debate of the possibility and consequences of legalizing this institution of prostitution in the light of a brief argument of comparative nature, discussing the countries that have already legalized the same.

Key Words: *Prostitution, legalization of prostitution, world charter on prostitution, sex trafficking, ITPA.*

Introduction

Prostitution has a been looked at, with very hypocritical lenses. People who visit them actually enjoy it, but in society, they pretend otherwise. The encyclopedia of social science has brought up the most relevant interpretation "as the practice in which a female offers her body for promiscuous sexual intercourse for hire, for a consideration." But in the same context the enactment for Prevention of Immoral Traffic1 has defined prostitution as "Sexual exploitation or abuse of persons for commercial purposes."

Historical Existence of Prostituion

As per the Indian historical records, prostitution has remained in existence from time immemorial. There has been reference of the same in n number of Indian literatures. In fact, the Hindu mythology even the celestial demigods haven't been exempted from this ideology, for instance Menaka, Rambha, Urvashi, and Thilothamma. There are evidences traced in the works of the Mahakavi Kalidas that in prominent temples such as the Mahakala of Ujjain, prostitution was given a religious glaze to it. The women who were the sex workers here mostly comprised of girls who were donated to the shrine and the temple by the parents as a goodwill gesture to their religion and trying to fulfill their share of sacrificial duties that they are bound to by the prescription of the religion. They are termed as the Devadasi and Mukhies in south and north respectively.[2]

Women and wine were looked at with materialistic value than life during the medieval period. A royal patronage was given to sex workers as encouragement, probably leaving only Aurangazeb exception to this system. This era saw the rise of the systems of 'Tawaif' and 'Mujra'. These systems were more or less annexed to the concept of performing arts. To exhibit his authority and supremacy as extravaganza Emperor Jahangir chose means of having 6,000 mistresses. With the recession of the empire of the Mughal, the royal position and elite charms of this profession faded away. Since these women had exclusive training in only endowing sexual pleasures and weren't professing any other livelihood, placing them back to the society was next to impossible. Hence, they were forced to go back to the only thing they knew, thus becoming sex workers for perpetuity.

Though the British Raj, brought an improved life for women, it had no impact on the lives of these women. Rather it only got commercialized further. They were more vulnerable and victimized as well coerced into continuing in these professions and not swapping even if they wanted to fend for themselves via some other profession.[3]

In recent times, there has been a rise of notion that if prostitution is legalized, then there could be a considerable reduction and maybe some day complete eviction of the evils against women of our society. The urge of carnal desires of the men in a patriarchal country as ours there needs to be curbing of the same which is the root cause of the continuously rising harassment rates against women. The National Commission for Women and various other eminent women activists Lalitha Kumaramangalam has said she is strongly in favour of legalizing prostitution. She said it would lead to "easier control of the situation in which paid sex takes place."[4] Mamata Sharma who held the chair of the chief of NCW earlier backed the view of Lalitha Kumaramangalam. All the same Lalitha Kumaramangalam doesn't agree to the notion that this has got to do anything with the rape rates reducing consequently. She substantiated her disagreement with facts and figures stating that the closure of brothels in 1959, Queensland, in Australia, experienced a 149% increase in incidents of rape. Sex workers are the most marginalized members of society. They need protection and help. Legalizing the profession has multiple benefits.

Contributive Agents to Prostitution

It is difficult to mention the factors affecting prostitution as it is deep rooted in the society. Even though the most cited reason amongst all is the social and economic delegation of women by men.

Research states that following factors are favourable to prostitution:

1. Abduction: One of the most general cause. Studies says that many young girls are abducted from remote villages and while going to movies, cities, temples and marriages and exploiting their innocence. Most of them are abducted by females ad couples. About 35% of prostitution happens from abduction.
2. Devadasi System: the prostitution with religious sanction through inhuman system of Sevadasi System. Still it is there in a developing and democratic country like India. Girls are dedicated to goddess named 'Yellamma', in states of Karnataka and Maharashtra and become accessible to urban population after some time. So from this we can conclude that, economic arrangements, force and religious rituals are socialized instruments which decide the fate of a women. About 80% of total prostitution are Devadasis and 20% of the child prostitution legitimizing the practice of prostitution.
3. Rape: after the happening of rape, about 6% of girls enters into prostitution, the most cruel form of social stigma so that rape victims are not accepted in their home. As society is not ready to accept their existence, they find shelter in brothels. In some cases we can see that girls were sold by their own fathers, uncles and other relatives questioning the secrecy of relations.
4. Marriage: in Pune, about 15% of women in prostitution came from marriage.
5. Children of women in prostitution: invariably, female children of prostitutes finally ended up in

prostitution (98%) as there is no safe place for them for livelihood. This contributes about 10% of prostitution.

6. Social factors of prostitution : in Hindustan culture among Indians, women are considered as commodity. If women who had sex is considered as 'used goods'. Without a husband she is considered useless as an impoverished cultural outcast.

Following this fact, we can say that they has a useful place as a prostitute. Women who are widowed and divorced are also facing vast range of social stigma. If a women's husband died, she is not a virgin and remarriage is not accepted. In rural remote areas of India, "Johar", "Sathi', "Bride burning" etc is still prevailing. Because of the social stigma, women are forced to believe that they are useless after the marriage of her husband. When culture notions strongly came into force along with religion and poverty, more people will join prostitution.

Proverty's Role in Indian Prostitution

Even if India is a developing country, people has the most striking issue of poverty. 40% of India's population lives in poverty .i.e. about 400 million people do not have basic survival needs. Poverty does not have a gender and sexual difference. It increases vulnerability and provoke the existing power of people who are having gender prejudice. The problems faced by girls and women is a byproduct of patriarchal society. Domestic and caste issues reflects strong gender prejudice against women. Violence against women, sexual assault and rapes are not individual crimes. It is a tool for political statement for aggression and gender persecution, which reflects degree of human degradation and commoditization of women in society.

This desperate problem of poverty is considered as a root cause of growing prostitution. It is debatable that countries with high economy, education, high standards of living and equality of both sexes also have issues of prostitution. So this indicates that, mere illiteracy and poverty is not an issue of growing prostitution but people are consciously voluntarily choosing this occupation.

Torments Suffered By Prostitutes

Most of the workers are treated inhumanly at the early stages of their brothel life. They are manipulated and exploited and manipulated frequently to create fear. Most of the brothel owner, keep their prostitutes under house arrest preventing all possible way of escape. Small part of earning only will be given to them.

According to government estimates, among 3 million sex workers, most of them are HIV positive and suffering from various other diseases. They don't have access to proper medical treatment. Exploitation from male owners and customers. Law enforcing agencies are sitting blindly sitting and always take advantage of these people. They not only extract money but also abuse them physically and mentally.

Laws Addressing Sex Workers and Prostitution

Under Art.23 of the Indian Constitution, ban commercialization of women and girls through trafficking for sexual purpose and the second part of this Article declares that any contravention to this article will be punishable in accordance with existing law of land. Our state also have Special legislation such as Immoral Trafficking Act (ITPA), 1956 and other local legislation which implicitly as well as explicitly challenges the act of prostitution.

And at the same a person who attained majority and above, selling his or her body for sexual intercourse for money or for other purpose with opposite sex, 200 meters away the public places or any place notified by the government is not a crime under the Indian Penal Code,1860 or Under ITPA,1956.

Immoral Trafficking Act(ITPA)

The Immoral Trafficking (Suppression) Act was passed in the year of 1956 which was known to be SITA, where the sex workers allowed to ply their trade in private but they cannot carry out their business in the open or public places. The SITA 1956 has recently changed to become PITA or The Immoral Trafficking (Prevention) Act.

Cases registered under this Act has increased to 0.09% during the year of 2015. Most of the cases were registered under section 5 of ITP Act (1,287 cases), where the particular section deals with procuring or inducing or taking person for sole purpose of prostitution, and the issue under sec 5 is peak in Tamil Nadu, followed by Telangana (224 cases), Karnataka (207 cases) and Maharashtra (126 cases) and these four States comprises altogether 70.5% total such cases.

Certain section such as Sec 3 , Sec 2 and, Sec 5 under this Immoral Trafficking Act of 1956 emphasis on the statutory recognition on prostitution and on the restriction which put-forth by the legislature through this special legislation.

1. Punishment for keeping a Brothel or allowing premises to be used as a Brothel.[5]

(1) Any person who keeps or manages, or acts or assists in the keeping or management of, a brothel, shall be punishable on first conviction with rigorous imprisonment for a term of not less than one year and not more than three years and also with fine which may extend to two thousand rupees and in the event of a second or subsequent to conviction with rigorous imprisonment for a term of not less than two years and not more than five years and also with fine which may extend to two thousand rupees.

A any person who, -

(a) Being the tenant, lessee, occupier or person in charge of any premises, uses, or knowingly allows any other person to use, such premises or any part thereof as a brothel,

or

(b) Being the owner, lesser or landlord of any premises or the agent of such owner, lessor or landlord, lets the same or any part thereof with the knowledge that the same or any part thereof is intended to be used as a brothel, or is willfully a party to the use of such premises or any part there of as a brothel, shall be punishable on first conviction with imprisonment for a term which may extend to two years and with fine which fine which may extend to two thousand rupees and in the event of a second or subsequent conviction, with rigorous imprisonment for a term which may extend to five years and also with fine.

(2-A) For the purposes of sub-section (2), it shall be presumed, until the contrary is proved, that any person referred to in clause (a) or clause (b) of that subsection, is knowingly allowing the premises or any part thereof to be used as a brothel or, as the case may be, has knowledge that the premises or any part thereof are being used as a brothel, if, -

(a) A report is published in a newspaper having circulation in the area in which such person resides to the effect that the premises or any part thereof have been found to be used for prostitution as a result of a search made under this Act;

or

(b) A copy of the list of all things found during the search referred to in clause (a) is given to such person.

2. Procuring, inducing or taking person for the sake of prostitution.[6]

(1) Any person who-

(a) Procures or attempts to procure a person whether with or without his/her consent, for the purpose of prostitution; or

(b) Induces a person to go from any place, with the intent that he/she may for the purpose of prostitution become the inmate of, or frequent, a brothel; or

(c) Takes or attempts to take a person or causes a person to be taken, from one place to another with a view to his/her carrying on, or being brought up to carry on prostitution; or

(d) Causes or induces a person to carry on prostitution; shall be punishable on conviction with rigorous imprisonment for a term of not less than three years and not more than seven years and also with fine which may extend to two thousand rupees, and if any offence under this sub-section is committed against the will of any person, the punishment of imprisonment for a term of seven years shall extend to imprisonment for a term of fourteen years.

Provided that if the person in respect of whom an offence committed under this sub section, -

(i) Is a child, the punishment provided under this sub-section shall extend to rigorous imprisonment for a term of not less than seven years but may extend to life; and

(ii) Is a minor; the punishment provided under this sub-section shall extend to rigorous imprisonment for a term of not less than seven years and not more than fourteen years.

The sections above Sec3 as well Sec5 punishes the third party who either will be a mediator or will be the person induces to carry out the prostitution. Not in anyway these section affect the sex worker in comparison to the third party where the other section do not have any much variance in its effectiveness to the prostitution which can be held up same as in Sec3 as well Sec5.

The World Charter for Prostitutes Rights

World Charter for Prostitutes Right is a declaration which had been adopted in 1985 with the core object to protect the rights of the prostitutes. It was adopted by International Committee for Prostitutes (ICPR). This declaration states" all the prostitutes should be granted with human rights as well as all the civil liberties". World Charter also call up for providing working standard for prostitution where systematic zoning should be abolished. And all the acts of prostitution should be of individual decision, such act should not be punished or decriminalized.[7]

Panel to Monitor and Suggest Rehabilitation Scheme for Trafficked Sex Workers and Trafficked Victims

In case of Budhadev Karmaskar8, SC dissmiseed appeal by the accused in the case dealt with murder of a Sex Worker, the honourable SC held that the Central as well as the State Governments through Social Welfare Boards should prepare schemes for rehabilitation across the nation for physically and sexually abused women commonly known as the "prostitutes" as it is very much important to consider that even the prostitutes also have a right to live with dignity under Article 21 of the Constitution of India since they are also social animals born with dignity and their problems should be addressed. The Court also pointed a woman who indulged into prostitution not for sexual pleasure might turned out into sex worker because of the plight of poverty.

The Honourable Supreme Court of India directed both Central as well as State government to prepare resourceful schemes which should be implemented with core objective of the welfare of the sex workers and sexually abused women where their vocational skills in other areas of occupation should be developed . The scheme should be drafted by foreseeing the upcoming challenges and the question of how these schemes will rehabilitate them by settling the issues faced by those sex workers by offering other employment. Regarding this court issued notice to both Central and State Government.

The SC stated that "from a perusal of the UJAWALA Scheme it appears that the Central Government has a scheme only for rescued trafficked women but no scheme for those sex workers who voluntarily want to leave the sex trade. In our opinion, proper effective scheme should be prepared for such women also. In this connection, we would like to say that the Central Government Scheme has placed a condition that the rescued sex workers must stay in a corrective home in order to get technical training. In our opinion, no such condition should be imposed, as many sex workers are reluctant to stay in these corrective homes which they consider as virtual prison".

The Court also appointed a Panel of NGOs Activist and Lawyers to study, research and suggest a scheme in terms of:

(1) Prevention of trafficking,

(2) Rehabilitation of sex workers who wish to leave sex work, and

(3) Conditions conducive for sex workers who wish to continue working as sex workers with dignity.

Future Insights on Legalising Prostitution?

As the problem of prostitution is inevitable some people are of the opinion that prostitution should made legal in India and accept them as a part of our society. At least we can track the record of sex workers. Legalizing prostitution will be able to see the undercover business, gaining access to medical facilities, which can control the spread of AIDS. There is a need to treat sex industry as any other industry and to power up it with legal safeguards. The legalization will bring benefits sex workers and society as well. Keeping it illegal contributes to crimes such as robbery, fraud, rape etc because many criminals view the sex workers as a good targets. They are unlikely to report the crimes to police. If it is legal then they will easily go and report this police. Pros of legalizing of prostitution:

- Legalization of prostitution and the sex industry will seize women being abducted or trafficked for sexual commerce
- Legalization of prostitution will regulate the sex industry.
- Legalization of prostitution will reduce clandestine, hidden, illegal and street prostitution.
- Legalization of prostitution will protect the women in prostitution as they will have rights.
- Women in systems of Prostitution want the sex industry legalized as they are the one who suffers the most as they don't have any rights.
- Legalization of prostitution will promote women's health as they can have easy access to medical facilities which they don't have when it is illegal.
- Recognizing prostitution as an economic activity, thus enabling women in India to obtain working permits as "sex workers".

The question challenged before the peoples who have a optimistic views in legalizing prostitution is very basic. The questions which can be put-forth are:

- The scope of the term 'legalizing" whether the application of this term in the work of prostitution interpreted in a manner where the sex workers have a chance to have a brothel or sexual intersection by opposite sex at any place without any reasonable restriction, and proclaiming as such call girls are available between time to time?
- By upholding the legal acceptance of prostitution challenges the life of people. Wont the surrounding

will be safer and children are secured. And whether there will be a social acceptance on the fact renting a body for sexual pleasure which considered to be a perfect illegitimate activity.

- If major proportion of the Indian population does not want prostitution to be legalized, the only way to agree upon the legalization is to operate prostitution in specially designated area such as red-light district. Brothel can make registered which work under reasonable restriction imposed by statutory authority.
- The individuals involved in this nexus of prostitution, for all practical reasons avoid their involvement being publicly known. Most of them trying to mask their actual activities. Women from the high society participate in this covertly, often camouflaging their actions underneath some other profession. In such scenarios, how can the legal system of the country intervene? Do the laws of the country enable an individual or group of persons to demand the eradication of a brothel or brothel like institution such as the call center that is located in their neighborhood and be shifted to the permitted limits, or request actions against a person who runs the same in such an area? If not, then do the citizens under the pretext of "respecting" the rights of sex workers to an occupation of their choice and encourage their presence, thereby endanger their own lives?
- An answer is expected from the section of people who advocate the notion that sex workers need to be esteemed and not disgraced, as to who is to ensure the giving of "respect" to these women? Does the government have anything to do with curbing this? Can they take deterrent actions to prevent these incidents like how they coined rules to abolish untouchability? In case of untouchability,

one can prove progress by observing the increased rates of intermixing and interactions of the individuals in the society, by what can be evidentiary enough to show eradication of prostitution?

Conclusion

After analyzing from all the afore mentioned perspectives on this issue, a conclusion can be drawn that there can be accurate antidote or countermeasure for prostitution and all its allies that form the social evils for instance, criminalization, decriminalization or legalization. The only solution, possibly, that one can arrive at is women and men broadening their mindsets and recognizing the other gender and respecting the same and consider one another equal on all social parameters.

Notes

1. S. 2 (f) of the Prevention of Immoral Traffic Act-1987.
2. Pallavi Thakur, Tradition of Devadasi: The sacred prostitute!, SPEAKING TREE, Last accessed on 01/ march/2019 https://www.speakingtree.in/allslides/prostitution-in-ancient-india
3. Women's Social, Economic Inequality Leads To Trafficking, Domestic Violence, Exploitation, Say Speakers In Women's Commission, Forty-seventh Session, UN Meetings coverage and press release, 2003.
4. Smriti Kak Ramachandran, NCW chief for legalizing sex trade, THE HINDU, OCTOBER 28, 2014 00:59.
5. S.3 OF ITPA, 1956.
6. S.5 of ITPA, 1956.
7. International committee on the rights of prostitutes of Europe,2002 last accessed on 04/march/2019 https://www.walnet.org/csis/groups/icpr_charter.html
8. Budhadev Karmaskar v. State of West Bengal, (2011) 11 SCC 538.

20

Socio-Economic Status of Female Manual Labor Employees at Government Institute

— ***Parvoti Boli***

Abstract

The present study is an attempt to understand the socio-economic status and challenges faced by the Female Manual Labor Employees and how the women are empowered by their work. The population of the study comprise of all the female manual labor employees including cook, kitchen attendant, sweepers and gardeners. However, the study has considered only those female employees working at various hostels (both men and ladies) of the Rajiv Gandhi University, Itanagar, Arunachal Pradesh. The study has been made on the basis of primary data collected with the help of questionnaire and the simple frequency tables were used for data analysis. Stratified Random Sampling Technique was used by covering 50% of population irrespective of the type of their work. The findings of the study revealed that most of the women undertaken for the study enjoy equal status in their household and are equally involved in decision making process. Likewise, Widows and Unmarried women were found to be the breadwinner of the family and their monthly income is not sufficient for the family expenses. The study also reveals that majority of the women were forced to do this work by the situations in order to earn the living. Nevertheless, women are satisfied with their work as they are economically independent and are happy to contribute to the family income. Therefore, by observing the findings of the study we can conclude that though the earnings of these women might be insufficient for their daily expenses, they got the opportunity to work outside instead of solely confined to the household activities. Thus, they are somehow socially and economically empowered.

Keywords: *Socio-Economic Status, Challenges, Empowerment, Female, Manual Labor.*

Introduction

The term socio-economic status is used to describe an individual's or family's social and economic position in relation to others, based on occupation, education and income. Thus, the socio-economic status of women is the combined total measure of women's economic and social position. It is generally comprise not only income but also financial security, educational attainment, quality of life and involvement of women in decision making process.

The socio-economic status of women is of worth mentioning because women are more susceptible to social and economic disadvantage. In other words, being in the patriarchy society, women are vulnerable to unemployment, unsupportive education, lag in decision making process, violence against women and less participation in various social activities. These situations are generalized as a common case of low class women which can be associated with poverty. Because, it is believe that in compare to low class women, high class women have more privilege of education, freedom of employment and most importantly their involvement in decision making in the household. Furuta and Salway (2006) stated that in Nepal, women who were employed were more likely to participate in all aspects of decision-making than those who were not employed. Similarly, highly educated women and those living in the richest households were more likely to state their views on all aspects of decision making (Acharya et. al. 2010).

Nevertheless, poverty is not only the sole cause for an underprivileged of women, but it may also be associated with the rigidity in the culture, religion, community and patriarchy. Masarat and Kawale (2017) reported that

Muslim women are prevented from participating in developmental activities and they do not want to educate their daughters beyond the primary level of education in order to safeguard the community identities. Further, many middle class women particularly Muslim women in India, who have requisite qualifications are not allowed to seek employment because 'community respectability' is likely to get smeared (Engineer 2005).

The female manual labor employees of Rajiv Gandhi University are the lowest wage earner among the officially appointed employees in the institute except for those regular employees. However, the study undertaken is only confined to the manual employees at the hostels (both men and women) of the University. It comprised all type of manual workers such as kitchen attendant, cook, sweepers and gardeners. The work of cook and kitchen attendant are confined within the kitchen and dining, particularly engaged in cooking, washing of dishes and cleaning of dining and kitchen. The second group is mainly engaged in cleaning of entire building including bathroom. And the third group is engaged only in gardening. The present study is an attempt to investigate the socio-economic status of these female manual employees and the daily challenges faced by them.

Objectives of the study

1. To study the social status of the female manual labor employees.
2. To understand the economic condition of the female workers.
3. To examine the daily challenges face by them.

Delimitation

1. The female manual labor employees.
2. Hostels (both men and women) of Rajiv Gandhi University.
3. Socio-economic status and challenges.

Methodology of the study

- **Method:** Interview method was used with the help of questionnaire. Simple frequency tables were constructed for the analysis of data.
- **Population:** All the female manual labor employees at the hostels of Rajiv Gandhi University.
- **Sample:** Stratified Random Sampling technique was used and thereby 21 female employees were selected as sample covering 50 percent from the population of approximately 42.

Analysis and Interpretation

Table 1: Age Structure of the Female Manual Labor Employees

Sl. No.	*Age*	*No. of Respondents*	*Percentage*
1	Below 20 years	0	0
2	20-35 years	16	76.2
3	35-50 Years	5	23.8
4	Above 50 years	0	0
	Total	**21**	

Source: Primary Data.

Interpretation: From the above table it is seen that the majority i.e. 76.2 % female manual employees are under the age group of 20-35 years. Similarly, 23.8% of female manual employees are under the age group of 35-50 years and there is not a single employee under the age group of below 20 years and above 50 Years.

Table 2: Educational Background of the Female Manual Employees

Sl. No.	Qualification	No. of Respondents	Percentage
1	Graduate and above	0	0
2	Higher Secondary	2	9.5
3	Secondary	5	23.8
4	Middle	7	33.3
5	Primary	7	33.3
6	Illiterate	0	0
	Total	**21**	

Source: Primary Data.

Interpretation: The above table shows that only 9.5 % of the female manual employees are educated up to higher secondary level (10+2) and 23.8 % are educated up to secondary level (matriculation).While, 66.7% of the female manual employees were below matriculation at the time of joining in their respective job. Interestingly, there is no illiterate and graduate employee among the population.

Table 3: Marital Status of the Female Manual Employees

Sl. No.	*Status*	*No. of Respondents*	*Percentage*
1	Married	15	71.4
2	Unmarried	2	9.5
3	Widow	4	19
	Total	**21**	

Source: Primary Data.

Interpretation: It is clear from the above table that the majority i.e. 71.4% of the female manual employees are married, while only 9.5% are unmarried. At the same time, 19% of the female employees are widow.

Table 4: The Places these Female Employees have come from

Sl. No.	*Areas*	*No. of Respondents*	*Percentage*
1	From Rural Areas	15	71.4
2	Small Town	6	28.6
3	Large town	0	0
	Total	**21**	

Source: Primary Data.

Interpretation: Based on the collected data it is revealed that out of all the respondents, 71.4% of female employees have come from rural areas. Similarly, 28.6% of employees have come from small towns. However, no female employees have come from other large town or have been living in the present place from the beginning. They have moved from one place or the other, including both rural areas and small towns to the present place, travelling a considerate distance between their place of origin and the place of working.

Table 5: Reasons for moving to the present place

Sl. No.	Reasons	No. of Respondents	Percentage
1	More job opportunities	2	9.5
2	Got a job	9	42.8
3	Marriage	10	47.6
	Total	**21**	

Source: Primary Data

Interpretation: When asked about the reasons for moving into the present place, 47.6% of the employees responded that they have moved to the present place due to their marriage. In the same way, 42.8% have moved after getting the job and only 9.5% of employees have moved in search of job.

Social Background of the Female Manual Labor Employees

Table 6: Social life of the Female Employees

Sl. No.	*Questions*	*Yes/Sometimes*		*No*	
		No. of Respondents	*Percentage*	*No. of Respondent*	*Percentage*
1	Do family support in working outside?	21	100	0	0
2	Do husband help with housework activities? (only for married women)	15	100	0	0
3	Do husband help with child care? (for married women)	15	100	0	0
4	Feel Safe at workplace?	21	100	0	0
5	Ever encountered any kind of harassment from male counterparts or employer?	0	0	21	100
6	Ever faced domestic violence	3	14.2	18	85.7
7	Ever bullied by the locality due to status of work?	1	4.8	20	95.2

Source: Primary Data.

Interpretation: According to the analyzed data, it is observed that 100% of the female employees are supported by the family for their working outside. When asked to the married women whether the husband help with housework and the child care? 100% of married women responded sometimes and both the husband and wife are equally engaged in child care. It is also found that all the employees feel safe at their workplace and no one had ever encountered any kind of harassment from their male counterparts. Among the employees, 14.2% of respondents have been a victim of domestic violence, while 85.7% of respondents are free from domestic violence. Similarly, only 4.8% of the employees are bullied by their locality due to the status of their work while, the remaining 95.2% have not faced such disrespectful act against them.

Table 7: Decision Making Authority of the Women

Sl. No.	Questions	Me		Husband/ parents		Both	
		No.	(%)	No.	(%)	No.	(%)
1	Decision of working outside	19	90.5	0	0	2	9.5
2	Decision of buying household assets	9	42.8	2	9.5	10	47.6
3	Children Education	4	100	0	0	15	100
4	Personal Expenses	17	80.9	0	0	4	19
5	Expenses on children	13	68.4	0	0	6	31.6

Interpretation: From the collected data it is found that 90.5% of the female employees have freedom of making their own decision about working outside and only 9.5% have said that the decision of working outside was made by both husband and wife. The data also shows that in the decision making process of children education both are equally engaged i.e. 100% excluding the widows for whom there is no involvement of husband in decision making. In the same way, 68.4% of women make the decision about children expenses and the remaining 31.6 % are made by both. In the decision of buying household assets 42.8% respondents are involved while, 47.6% involved both. It is good to know from the table that, in the personal expenses of women about 80% have freedom of making own decision.

Economic Condition of the Female Manual Labor Employees

Table 8: Economic Condition of the women

Sl. No.	*Questions*	*Yes/sometimes*		*No*	
		No. of Respondents	*Percentage*	*No. of Respondents*	*Percentage*
1	Is job permanent?	1	4.8	20	95.2
2	Is the only person earning in the family?	8	38.1	13	61.9
3	Is an earning sufficient for family expenses?	1	4.8	20	95.2
4	Have any other source of earning?	0	0	21	100
5	Whether satisfied with job?	11	52.4	10	47.6
6	Whether feel that salary is little low in compare to work?	20	95.2	1	4.8

Source: Primary Data.

Interpretation: The above table reveals that job of only 4.8% of the female employee is regular and the rest of 95.2% are not regular. Among the respondents 38.1% are the only person earning in the family which mainly includes widows, unmarried women and few of married women. However, 61.9%, especially married women are not the only breadwinner of the family since their husbands are equally contributing in their family income. When asked about whether their income is sufficient for daily family expenses and medical expenses, 95.2% of the employee's responses were negative and 4.8% responses were positive. From the above table it is also observed that no female employees have other source of earning other than their job. Out of all the respondents 52.4% are satisfied with their job despite of not being sufficient for the family expenses and other 47.6% were not satisfied with their job. Similarly, when asked whether they feel their salary is too low in compare to their workload, 95.2% responses were positive and only 4.8% responses were negative.

Table 9: Duration of the job and monthly income of the women:

Sl. No.	*Duration*	*No.*	*Percentage*	*Monthly Income*
1	Less than 1 year	5	23.8	7000
2	1-10 years	13	61.9	7000-8000
3	Above 10 years	3	14.3	9000-27000
	Total	21		

Source: Primary Data.

Interpretation: The above table shows that the duration of 23.8% of employees is less than 1 year and 61.9% employees are under 1-10 years. Only 14.3% of the employees have been working for more than 10 years. It is also clear from the table that the salary of employees increased with the increasing duration of work.

Table 10: Reasons for joining the job

Sl. No.	*Reasons*	*No. of respondents*	*Percentage*
1	I like this work	2	9.5
2	I am not qualified for any other job	7	33.3
3	I am forced to do this job to earn my living	11	52.4
4	To contribute to the family income	4	19.0
5	I want to be economically independent	3	14.3
6	Other	0	0

Source: Primary Data.

Interpretation: It is observed from the collected data that the majority i.e. 52.4% employees are working under compulsion in order to earn their living. Whereas, only 9.5% employees responded that they like the work and the other 19.0% have joined the job to contribute to family income. The remaining 14.3% have joined to become economically independent.

Challenges faced by the female employees

Based on collected data it has been found that the employees have to work for 6-7 hours daily which is followed by the time table; Morning- from 6.30 am to 9 am, Noon-11am to 12.30 pm and Evening- from 6.30 pm to 9 pm. However, this time table is exempted for those gardener and sweepers who work from morning 9 to 12 pm. It has also found that all the women still have to work rigorously at home even after coming back from their tiresome work. When asked what they mostly don't like about their work? The majority of the women employees replied because of the clashes of timing of their home and the work place, while according to some of the respondents, they mostly don't like the work because of the high work load.

Findings of the Study

1. The results of the study demonstrate that the middle aged women i.e. 20-50 years are mostly engaged in this work.
2. The educational background of the women seems to play a major role for entering into this work, since, the majority of female employees were educated below matriculation. And the married women are more likely to engage in this work.
3. It has found that most of the women have migrated from rural areas to the present location mainly due to marriage as well as after getting the job.
4. The findings of the study reveal that the women enjoy equal status at their household as they are equally involved in decision making process of household. They have the freedom of making their own decision about working outside and are fully supported by the family.
5. Except for a meager number, most of the women have not been victimized to domestic violence and they feel safe at their workplace. It shows that

gender biasness hardly exists at their household as well as at workplace.

6. The job of 95% of female employees is not regular as a result they get lower salary than those of 5% regular employees.
7. Widows and unmarried women are found to be the breadwinner of the family.
8. By considering their educational background majority of the women were satisfied with their job, though their earning were not sufficient for family expenses.
9. The majority of the women employees feel that their salary is little low in compare to their work.
10. It has found that the salary of the employees increased with increasing duration of the work and they may be regularized by fulfilling the minimum qualification.
11. The study also found that majority of women were forced by some unavoidable situations to do this work in order to earn the living.
12. After coming back from tiresome work all the women still work at their respective home as they think it is the duty of the women.

Conclusion

By observing the findings of the study we can conclude that though the earnings of these women might be insufficient for their daily expenses, they got the opportunity to work outside instead of solely confined to the household activities. In addition, they are equally working outside like those of male counterparts, and earning and contributing equally to their household income. Thus, they are somehow socially and economically empowered. When asked if they need any kind of changes in their work, the female manual employees responded that they are satisfied with their work, but increase in salary and regularizing their respective job would help in further improvement of their economic conditions. Therefore, the Govt. may look into the matter and take significant steps towards it.

References

Acharya, D.R., Bell, J.S., Simkhada, P., Teijlingen, E.R.V. & Regmi, P.R. (2010). "Women's Autonomy in Household Decision-Making: A Demographic Study in Nepal. Reproductive Health 7(15).

Engineer, A. A. (2005). Islam Women and Gender Justice, New Delhi, Kalpaz Publisher.

Furuta, M. & Salway, S. (2006). "Women's Position within the Household as a Determinant of Maternal Health Care Use in Nepal." International Family Planning Perspectives 32(1): 17–27.

Masarat, A. & Kawale, L. (2017). A Sociological Study on Freedom, Economic Independence and Decision Making among Muslim Women in Kalabuagi District. Excellence International Journal of Education and Research ISSN 2349-8838. Vol. 4. No. 7. July 2017. P. 77-90.

Pambè, M.W., Gnoumou, B., Kaboré, I. (2013). Relationship between Women's Socio Economic Status and Empowerment in Burkina Faso: A focus on Participation in Decision Making and Experience of Domestic Violence. United State Agency International Development. August. No. 99.

21

Barriers Faced by Elderly Women Destitudes–An Insight into the Psycho-social Issues A Case Study on ST Joseph Hospice, Mettur, Dindigul District.

— *Shella Mathu vatheni*

Introduction

Old people are the most respectful and sensitive people on this planet. They ought to be revered and taken care of by the younger members of the family. However, most of them are neglected and are left to fend themselves. According to Population Census 2011 there are nearly 104 million elderly persons in India; 53 million females and 51 million males. While the southern states (Andhra Pradesh, Karnataka, Kerala, and Tamil Nadu) may be considered the biggest drivers of aging in India, other Indian states (notably Haryana, Himachal Pradesh, Maharashtra, Orissa, and Punjab) are also experiencing an elderly population boom, largely in rural areas. An analysis of morbidity patterns by age clearly indicates that the elderly experience a greater burden of ailments compared to other age groups across genders and residential locations. The elderly most frequently suffer from cardiovascular illness, circulatory diseases, and cancers, while the non-elderly face a higher risk of mortality from infectious and parasitic diseases.

The Constitution of India, in Article 41 of the Directive Principles of State Policy specifies that the state shall within the limits of its economic policy provide for assistance to the elderly. National Old age Pension Scheme (NOAP) was introduced by the Indian government to provide Rupees 200 per month to the old and destitute people. Despite all the policies and benefits from the government old age people still undergoes social and pshycological barriers. As these people becomes fragile and dependent due to their age they were facing denial, a perceived lack of social support, a lack of knowledge or a dysfunctional attitude from their family members, in the present context they were disown by their own family members made them to stay on road and indulge in begging and other cheap activities.

Psycho-social Issues Faced by Elderly Women Destitudes

Though fulfillment of basic needs is essential for the survival of mankind yet man as a social being, does not live by bread alone. He wants to live in the society where he gets the feeling of belongingness. Such associations give meaning to his life. He occupies some position and enjoys some privileges, performs useful functions for the society. In the traditional Indian society, the aged persons were given deference and they enjoyed position of authority. In return, they used to provide guidance to the younger generation because age was equated with knowledge and experience. Displacement of folk knowledge with the scientific knowledge in the modern society has lowered their status to such an extent that economically, inactive and old persons is treated as a burden on the limited resources of the family. Such a situation has created a feeling of neglect, dependency, loneliness, powerlessness, meaninglessness and abondmentamong the poor old persons.

The situation becomes still worse if the old couples have to live alone by themselves in roads by begging and it becomes unbearable, if one of them is a chronic patient or dead. This sort of situation may happen with the rich elderly persons also who have been deserted by their sons on roads as they found them as disturbance and in some cases old people volunterly comes out from their family due to intolerance of abusive words and illtreatment that leaving the old parents to suffer psychological trauma silently.

The elder people who were disowned by their own family won't have permanent place of shelter so they will sleep in some common places like bustands, railway stations, in front of churches and temples but there are possibilities for them to facephysical abusive from that area goons and sometimes from police officers. Before people had some courtesy to send their old parents to old age homes, where old age homes has became many but presently hospice getting evolved in order to take care of destitudes.

Review of Literature

Warnick,1995 explains Aging as a series of processes that begin with life and continue throughout the life cycle. It represents the closing period in the lifespan, a time when the individual looks back on life, lives on past accomplishments and begins to finish off his life course. Adjusting to the changes that accompany old age requires that an individual is flexible and develops new coping skills to adapt to the changes that are common to this time in their lives.

Penninx et al., 1998 explains the nature of Depressive symptoms in old age people is not only have an important place as indicators of psychological well-being but are also recognized as significant predictors of functional health and longevity. Longitudinal studies demonstrate that increased depressive symptoms are significantly associated with increased difficulties in life of elder people with activities of daily living.

Pasco & Pinellas 2013 explains Aging as a process of growing old. It is a normal phenomenon which includes growth and maturity of the body. There are many physical and psychological changes in the process of aging or growing old. These changes are not harmful but bodily function is gradually being decline.

Traphagan, John W 2004 explains the physical and psychological changes inelderly, there is also a great chance of suicidal case. They can attempt suicide because of depression and loneliness also. Problem with memory make them difficult to remember simple things what happened just earlier. For instance, the day's new events, what was eaten for breakfast, dates. Memory generally declines with age. Lots of things go up and down during this stage of life.

Jacqui Allen and Peter Feldman (2013) did a systematic narrative review of consumer directed care for older people. They had the conclusion that consumer-directed care has the potential to empower older people and their caregivers by offering them greater flexibility and by increasing their involvement in case-related decisions.

Methodology

General Objective

The main objective of the study is to understand the treatment, preference and attitude that they are receiving from the society after they disowned by their family.

Specific Objectives

1. To examine the socio economic and psychological background of the elder people.
2. To study the struggles faced by them to lead their life in hospice.

3. To analyses the circumstance that make them to leave their family.
4. To find out the source of strength which helps them to deal with their day today psycho-social problems.
5. To understand the institutional care and support for elderly destitutes at St. Joseph Hospice

Concepts

Destitudes

Destitudes are the one who don't possess the necessaries of life in a condition of want needy.

Hospice

Hospice is a place where a type of care and philosophy of care that focuses on the palliation of a chronically ill, terminally ill or seriously ill patient's pain and symptoms, and attending to their emotional and spiritual needs.

Variables

Dependent: status, circumstances, extend of care and support, life of destitudes

Independent: Age, gender, Psycho-social status

Case Study

Based on purposive interview a case study was conducted on 15 women destitudes who are staying in St. Joseph Hospice, Mettur, Dindigul district.

Tool

Unstructured interview schedule

Source of Data Collection

Primary data is collected through personal interview from the respondents in face to face interaction.

Secondary data is collected from published books like magazine, articles, internet, websites etc.

Findings

- From the 30 elderly destitudes majority of them belongs to hindu community and were from middle class family mainly widows who were disown their own son because of the misunderstanding happened with their daughter in law's.
- Two destitudes are from north India who were take by their family for a tour to Madurai and Dindigul left them in the road and gone back without taking them were admitted in the hospice by the police.
- Four destitudes explained the mistreatment and ignorance they faced in the family after their wife's death which made them to come out of the house
- In them 7 elders had did their primary education and did descent jobs in the past but now due to the health complications they can't do anything but begging.
- While interacting with women elders they came up with unique stories in it Mrs. Lakshmi who got married at the age of 15 and lost her husband in the age of 20 suffered a lot to bring her only son to good position but once he get married he started to ignore her she had a health issue of low pressure that made her to faint often, so her son admitted her in the government hospital and never returned so she was sent to hospice by the doctors, still she believes of her son's arrival and take her back.
- Another Elder man Mrs. Rajalakshmi said after she met with an accident and became bedridden his daughter found it hard to take care of him so she forcefully admitted him in the hospice.

Suggestions

1. NGO's should identify the destituted elders in the street and should admit them in the old age homes or hospices
2. Awareness program should be conducted about the importance of elderly care
3. Health camp should be conducted frequently at hospice.
4. Proper counseling should be given to the elders admitted in the hospice
5. People who abuse elders should be punished.

Conclusion

Feeling different or awkward may lead to isolation or to an inability to care about others. There was an underlying discourse relating to how the participants believed society viewed the elderly as a group of citizens. A view needs to be altered in favor of a more positive image of elderly people. The social view of elderly people should be more positive to give them feeling of belonging. The difficulties caused by decreased physical condition for elderly persons should be understood. "Altered doings" illustrate how the doings have changed. When participants could no longer carry out activities in the same way as previously, they found a new way to perform the activity or did it in the same way but took pause. Helping elderly people get motivation to continue living at home could make them be active and keep doing things when it is possible. It may help to reduce the problems about shortage of social services for elderly people.

Biblography

https://www.who.int/ageing/projects/elder

https://www.helpageindia.org/our-work/welfare-development/old-age-homes

https://www.ncbi.nlm.nih.gov/pmc/articles

http://www.yourarticlelibrary.com/india-2/top-5-problems-faced-in-old-age/47679

www.questjournals.org/jrhss/papers/vol3-issue3/I335254.pdf

22

Visions of Dr. B.R. Ambedkar in the Emancipation of Tribes in India: Discourse on the Inefficient Interference of Institutions

— *Dr. Sukumaran. M &*
Dr. Santhosh Areekkuzhiyil

Abstract

The contribution of Dr. Ambedkar in the emancipation of dalits and Tribes in India is very significant in the historical legacy of transformation of tribes and dalits in India. The concerted efforts of Ambedkar have been benefited to the tribes and dalits in India to liberate from many of the legal, social, political and economic restrictions at a large extent. The results mostly reflected in socio-economic, political and legal arenas of tribal and dalit population in India. The immense contribution of Ambedkar has paved the way for the culmination of social justice compared to the olden days. This paper theoretically explains the reason behind the least effectiveness of constitutional provisions envisaged in the Indian constitution for social justice. It also presents some of the lived experiences and socio-political theories to explain the discrepancies existing in social justice of the tribes in India.

Keywords: *Ambedkar Vision, Emancipation, Tribes, institutional bottlenecks.*

1. Introduction

The contribution of Dr. Ambedkar in the emancipation of dalits and Tribes in India is very significant in the historical legacy of tribes and dalit transition in India. The concerted efforts of Ambedkar have been benefited to the tribes and dalits in India to liberate from many of the legal, social, political and economic restrictions at a large extent. The result has been mostly reflected in socio-economic, political and legal avenues of the tribes and dalits population in India. The contribution of Ambedkar has paved the way for the culmination of social justice compared to the olden days. According to Ambedkar the term "social justice" is based upon equality, liberty and fraternity of all human beings. (Dr. Ambedkar's vision: "Social Justice" for the women, scheduled castes and scheduled tribes, P. 86.)

The aim of social justice is to remove all kinds of inequalities based upon Caste, race, sex, power, Position, and wealth. The social justice brings equal distribution of the social, political and economical resources of the community. But it is observed that even after the 70 years of enactment of constitution by incorporating special safeguards to the tribes and dalits, the vision and mission of Ambedkar on the emancipation of social groups has not been fully culminated, particularly scheduled castes and scheduled tribes. Moreover, social disturbance in the form of caste, tribe, power, position and wealth etc are still exists. The ineffective institutional interference in the implementation of constitutional provisions acts as a bottleneck in the emancipation of tribal population. In this juncture this paper is an attempt to discuss the convergence and divergence of current status of socio-economic emancipation of tribes in India in Ambedkar vision on social justice and emancipation. This paper traces the reason behind the least effectiveness of constitutional provisions envisaged in the Indian constitution for social justice. It also presents some of the lived experiences and socio-political theories to explain the discrepancies existing in social justice of the tribes in India.

2. Significance of the study

The weaker sections of the society particularly the scheduled caste and scheduled tribes in India has been undergoing ruthless human rights violation even after 60 years of declaration of human rights through the constitutional provision. In different parts of the nation, the marginalized communities are still in the clutches of human right violation even though the constitution of India envisages various socio economic and political provisions. This paper looks on the visions of Ambedkar on various aspects of emancipation of nation with special focus on the ground reality of tribes in Kerala and the role played by the institutions through its bureaucracy in the dilution of implementation of various development policies and programmes exclusively meant for tribal population. The paper will have a strong impetus on the future of policy making and implementation of various development policies exclusively meant for tribal population.

3. Methodology

The study followed the mixture of qualitative and historical methods. The data for the present paper has collected from the review of various articles and historical writings on Ambedkar and his visions in the emancipation of marginalised groups in the society particularly tribes in India. The results of reviews were triangulated with the empirical data and lived experiences.

4. Objectives' of the Paper

The paper has following objectives:

1. To have discourse on the visions of Dr. B.R. Ambedkar in the emancipation of tribes in India.
2. To highlight the institutional bottlenecks in the implementation of various developmental programmes on the tribes in India.

5. Review of literature and discussions

The review of related literature and discussions are presented in four heads namely: 1.Tribal integration visions and realities, 2. Visions on education development among the tribes and achievements, Visions on land reforms and present situation and 4.Tribal development approaches and achievements.

5.1. Tribal Integration visions and realities

Dr. B. R. Ambedkar was aware about the socio-economic and political backwardness of tribes in India who contribute about 7 percent of total population of the country. Ambedkar policy was to integrate the tribals with the larger society. His keen interest was to ensure building up of the required strength in the tribal people to meet the competitive situations by providing built-in special arrangements (Parthasarathy. J, 1992). The vision on the tribal integration was one of the most significant foresights made by Ambedkar for the all round development of the tribes in India. But, even after 60 years of great legacy of Ambedkar on the tribal integration, the tribes in India has been further segregated with the influence and interference of extraneous forces. The external forces are tirelessly working to stimulate the rivalry between the tribes. In many parts of India there exists a strong rivalry between the tribal communities. The inter tribal rivalry increase the deprivation of tribal population due to the dis integration. The dis integration will reduce the voice of the tribes as an integrated team at the same time the extraneous forces can take advantages of this gap. Let us familiarise the rivalry evolved between two tribal groups in Kerala.

In Kerala the Marati community at Hosdurg Taluk of Kasaragod district was included in the ST list as per the Scheduled castes Scheduled tribes list (Modification) order, 1956. As per the Scheduled Castes and Scheduled Tribes Orders (Amendment) Act, 2002 the Marati community was excluded from the list of Scheduled Tribes of Kerala and three tribes namely Mavilan, Malavettuvan and Karimbalan were included in the ST list. In 2012 the Registrar General of India recommended re-inclusion of Marati community in the Scheduled Tribes list of Kerala State on 02.02.2012. During these inclusion and exclusion process, a rivalry, instead of integration has been evolved among the tribal communities. In between these, political parties taking concerted efforts to widen the gap between the tribal groups since all the political parties anticipate equal threat in the integration of tribal communities.

5.2 Visions on education development among the tribes and achievements

Article 46 of Indian constitution states that: The state shall promote with special care the educational and economic interest of the weaker sections of the people in particular, of SCs and ST and shall protect them from social injustice and all forms of exploitation (Sherin et. al, n.d). In Ambedkar perception, the strategies for emancipating the weaker sections in the society was exclusively different from the development approaches that the governments have been following since the initiation of planning. Ambedkar vision on the development of tribal education laid up on the opening up of schools nearby the tribal inhabitation and selecting the best from them and supply higher education and send to the out of nation for getting standard education by providing scholarship. After acquiring higher education give placement to them in government offices. Thus the educational philosophy of Abedkar for marginalised segments in the society, particularly, scheduled tribes and scheduled caste is holistic. This was intended to strengthen the individual as well as the society by capturing bureaucratic power.

Nirmal Kumar, (1972:278). Analysed a statement of Ambedkar and concluded that,

> Dr. Br. Ambedkar is quite correct when he says that we should raise the status of backward classes as

whole and not individually; but that can only be done by producing highly qualified people from amongst these communities and placing them in key positions of Government services. (P. 278).

From this analytical conclusion, the vision and mission of Ambedkar for the educational development of tribes in India is very obvious. Ambedkar philosophy on the need and significance of education has far reaching foresight to enables the tribal individuals and society to ameliorate and bring in par with the others in the society. But the educational philosophy has not been yet come in to reality. Still many of the tribal population in India are illiterate. The literacy rate of tribal population in India is the worst among the various social groups. Around 25 percent of India's tribal population is still illiterate (Census, 2011). Only 13 percent of the population aged between 18-23 were enrolled in higher education, where the percentage of other social groups and total population in higher education is comparatively high. It constitutes 24 percent for total population (MHRD, 2016).

5.3. Ambedkar visions on Land Reforms and present status of tribes in India

Ambedkar's perspectives on the land reforms were entirely different from the historical legacy of land reforms and the present status of land holdings in India. It is very ridiculous to say that even after the 60 years of land reforms, many of the tribal people, the actual owners of the land are not having even a piece of land even to built a permanent house. According to Ambedkar Land reforms is the sum of consolidation of land, nationalization of land and collective farming, institutional and technological reforms (Sherin et. al, n.d). In Ambedkar perspectives the landless marginalized class will be the owner of the land. All these visions are taking care of the socio-economic, historical and political realities of tribes in India. Since the tribal community has been the most deprived, marginalized and vulnerable segments in the society tribal people in India deserves largely the ownership of the land. But still many of the tribal families in India are not having land holdings for their conventional agricultural practice and to earn their income for livelihood. In such a situation the lack of cultivable land places the tribal at the mercy of the non-tribal farmers. Positive correlation also exists between the proportion of household with no cultivable land (Kunhaman, 1985).

5.4. Tribal development approaches and achievements

The efforts to ameliorate the tribals in India have been started from first Five Year Plan (1951-56) onwards through special sector of development, namely welfare of backward classes. An integrated development of the tribal population was started in the second plan period by establishing special multipurpose Tribal Blocks (Parthasarathy, 1992). The efforts were enthusiastically continued till the sixth plan all the efforts are underpinned by the development perspectives of Ambedkar and his solutions for the development of weaker sections in the society. But even after 65 years of planned development strategies the gap between social groups continues. It is very pervasive in education, health, employment, land ownership, economic situation, social relation etc. The long term objectives of improving quality of life of the tribal people are also in cross roads. It is evident even in Kerala which is globally acknowledges as the model of development with higher literacy, education, standard of living even with low level of percapita income. "Kerala model" has been referred to as a paradox of social development and economic backwardness. It is often also argued that the "Kerala model" (Kerala Development Report, 2005). The health status of the tribes in India is very much evident: infant mortality rate is 47, child mortality 15, maternal mortality rate is 212 (Directorate of Health Services, 2012), about 36 percent of Indian tribal households are still deprived in basic amenities (Sukamaran, 2016). In the three Panchayath of Agali,

Pudur and Sholapur in Attapadi, there were 776 deaths and only 519 births between January 1, 2011, and June 30, 2012, according to RTI information. (Satheesh A, 2012).

5.5. Institutional Bottlenecks and Tribal Development

The institutions especially the political parties and the changing governments can play a decisive role in ensuring the development of tribal communities. The coalition politics and their respective government have been acting according to the identification and recommendation of political parties and party leaders. Since the tribal people are inefficient to influence the political parties and party leaders, permenantly the care of these institutions lacking. The bureaucratic behaviour towards the tribes and implementation of development programmes meant for tribal population have been not in accordance with the requirements. Thus many of the programmes met in to vain or the benefits of the programmes implemented have not been reached in to the actual beneficiaries. The analysis reveals that the majority of beneficiaries are of the opinion that government ignores the tribal society. Furthermore, there is not much participation in Rural Development Schemes by women of tribal areas and corruption prevails in Government machinery. The government officials are involved in the favouritism in selecting IRDP families and favouritism in selecting Rural Development Schemes beneficiaries (Rajneesh, 2014).

6. Findings

1. Ambedkar visions on tribal integration is not yet realized, instead segregation is more pervasive.
2. Ambedkar visions on the development of tribal education and equality in education is not yet fulfilled. The participation of tribes in higher education is only 13 percent.
3. There exists a wide gap between Ambedkar views on land reforms the ground reality of tribal land holdings in India.

4. Even after the 65 years of planned development, the human development of the tribes in India is still in cross roads.
5. The institutional bottlenecks acts as strong driving force in the failure of tribal development programmes in tribal population.

7. Conclusion

The results and discussions in the paper on the visions of Dr. Ambedkar in tribal emancipation based on the empirical evidences, and lived experiences, the paper could effectively portrayed the foresighted visions of Ambedkar in the emancipation of tribes in India. But the paper could found out that, there exists a wide gap between the holistic tribal emancipation philosophy of Ambedkar and the present ground reality. It is further haunting the thoughts and efforts of the social scientists and policy makers to bridge the existing gap in philosophy and reality. No doubt concerted efforts of the government and policy makers are some of the driving force which stimulate and accelerate the development trajectory of trial population in India in tune with the holistic philosophy of Dr. B.R. Ambedkar. More over the institutional bottlenecks acts as a strong factor which accelerates the human rights violation of tribes in India. Hope the timely supply and delivery of education would equip the tribal population in India to fulfil the visions of tribes in India (Rajneesh, 2014).

References

Satish, A. (2012). Hopless Existance of Attapadi Tribals. The New Indian Express, Palakkad Published: 07th September 2012 08:12 AM Last Updated: 07th September 2012.

Parthasarathay, J. (1992). Ambedkar and Social justice. Shashi, S.S(Ed.). New Delhi, Ministry of Information and Broad Casting, Government of India.

Sukumaran, M. (2017), Deprivation of basic amenities among the tribals and development experiences in India. Paper accepted for presentation in National conference on Transition from MDGs to SDGs: India's Achievements, Challenges and opportunities on 27th and 28th January 2017, Department of Economics, and Annamalai University.

Bose, Nirmal Kumar. (1972). *Anthropology and some Indian Problems, in Man in India.* Vol. 37, No. 3 July.

Kerala Development Report. (2005). Thiruvananthapuram, Government of Kerala. p. 8.

Kunhaman. (1985). Tribal Eocnomy of Kerala- An Intra Regional Analysis. Economic and Political Weekly. 20(11).

Dr.Ambedkar's vision: "Social Justice" for the women, scheduled castes and scheduled tribes. P.86.Retrieved from shodhganga. inflibnet.ac.in.

Sherin, Shubhangi, Biswa, Bhushan, Dhilip, Prasant & Sujit. (n.d). Dr. Baba Saheb Ambedkar's vision of India's Development: Implications on Dalit's socio-economic andpolitical status. Retrieved from http://docshare01.docshare.tips/files/4549/45493448.pdf

Census. (2011). Retrievedform.http://censusindia.gov.in/2011-common/censusdataonline.html.

Educational Statistics at a Glance. (2016). Ministry of Human Resource Development, Government of India.Retrieved from mhrd.gov.in/statist?...statistic.

Rajneesh. (2014). Impact of Various Rural Development Schemes: An Evaluation. *International Journal of Management Research and Business Strategy.* 3(2). p. 104. Retrieved from. http://www.ijmrbs.com.

Tazeem Akter. (2016). Dr. B.R. Ambedkar: His 'Subdued' Economic Visions. *International Journal of Innovative Research and Development.* 5(1).P.48. Retrieved from. www.ijird.com.

23

Social Development through Welfare Policies in Karnataka: Special Reference to Marriages Schemes

— *Mr. Raviraj H Nagaral*

Introduction

Social welfare refers to the general welfare of society. With sufficiently twelve sturdy assumptions, it are often such because the summation of the welfare of all the people within the society. In applied welfare economic science, like in cost benefit analysis, money-value estimates are usually used, significantly wherever income-distribution effects are factored into the analysis or appear unlikely to undercut the analysis. The capabilities approach to welfare argues that freedom – what people are unengaged to do or be - ought to be enclosed in welfare assessments and also the approach has been significantly influential in development policy circles wherever the stress on multidimensionality and freedom has formed the evolution of the Human Development Index. The Constitution of India provides sure special Constitutional safeguards for the welfare of regular Castes and regular Tribes and other weaker sections of the society, in order that they could take their rightful place in community. As citizens of the Republic of India, they're absolutely entitled to sure rights and privileges, which were denied to them within the past on the bottom of Caste system and also the observe of Untouchability. Keeping seeable, the Constitutional mandate, The Government of Mysore, through financial aid Department, developed varied programmes and schemes for the upliftment of regular Castes and regular Tribes particularly for his or her socioeconomic and educational advancement from the year 1956 forwards.

Karnataka is considered as a model state in terms of social welfare and economic development in the country. The state government has implemented several schemes for the welfare of the citizens. The various welfare measures have been introduced under the respective State Departments.

The Karnataka State Government has introduced various measures such as educational schemes, financial awards, scholarships, grants, loans and fellowships of school education, literacy, higher education, elementary education, secondary education, technical education, medical education, tribal education, adult education and vocational studies under the Karnataka Education Department. These measures have been initiated to benefit all students of PhD, postgraduate (PG) and undergraduate (UG) courses. Students studying in classes IX, X, XI and class XII can also draw benefit from these educational schemes and programmes. These welfare measures are meant for general category students as well as for students categorized under Scheduled Castes (SC), Scheduled Tribes (ST), Other Backward Classes (OBC), minority category, disabled/physically handicapped, students from rural areas, and of Below Poverty Line (BPL). The main objectives of the educational schemes and programmes are to provide encouragement to students, to develop and upgrade skills, and to improve educational and economic status.

The Department of Women and Child Development under the Karnataka State Government has been assigned the responsibility to implement various social welfare schemes, including health and nutrition programmes for women and children. Various women and child welfare initiatives have been introduced to benefit pregnant women, mothers, girl children, nursing women, lactating mothers, widows, physically handicapped women, and old aged women. These schemes are also meant to benefit women Self-help Group (SHG), Anganwadi workers, women health volunteers, and women entrepreneurs. The main objectives of the women and child-welfare programmes are the to encourage and promote women empowerment, to promote gender equality, to ensure fulfillment of social, political, and economic rights of women, to protect women from all kinds of domestic violence, to protect and empower girl child, and to improve child sex ratio.

The State Government of Karnataka has established the Karnataka Labour Welfare Board to administer the labour welfare schemes in the state. The state government has constituted the Karnataka Labour Welfare Fund to promote and finance activities for the welfare of the employees. The main objectives of the labour welfare programmes are to enforce various labour laws and rules, to prevent strikes and lockouts, to settle industrial disputes arising out of lockouts, closures, strikes, layoffs, termination etc and to settle claims and matters related to workmen's compensation, gratuity, minimum wages, etc. Implementing various schemes of Central and State governments introduced for the welfare of the unorganized and organized workers, dealing with matters related to women workers, promoting worker's education scheme, and enforcing recreational activities for workers through various welfare centers also performed.

The Karnataka State Government recognizes that good health of its citizens is vital for the overall development of the state. To enhance the health and well-being of its people, the state government has implemented various health and family welfare schemes and programmes. These welfare schemes by Karnataka Government are aimed at reducing the suffering and ill health of people and in turn, improve their productivity. Facilities have been provided in all medical institutions of the state for conducting laparoscopic operations, IUD placements, tubectomy, and vasectomy. The main objectives of the health and family welfare schemes are to provide integrated and comprehensive primary health care, to improve health of all sectors of the society, to ensure even distribution of quality health care services, to control epidemics and outbreaks, to provide access to safe and quality drugs at affordable prices, and to increase access to systems of alternative medicine.

The Karnataka State Government has introduced several welfare schemes to benefit people with disabilities. The welfare schemes for disabled people are meant to facilitate the integration of such people in the mainstream of society. Through the Karnataka State Policy of Disability and the welfare schemes, the state government aims to safeguard the rights of people with disabilities. The main objectives of Karnataka Government's welfare programs for the disabled, people are to ensure rehabilitation for people with disabilities, and to provide education and economic opportunities for disabled people.

Review of Literature

Malik and Courtney (2011) studied that how higher education offers empowerment to women. The economic independence and increased standing with the family were the benefits of higher education. It also enabled the women to impact the discriminatory practices.

Rashmi Rani Agnihotri H. R et. al. (2017) study on "A Study on Women Empowerment Programmes in Karnataka State: A Theoretical Overview". This study discussed women empowerment programmes in Karnataka. The study found that empowerment of rural women can be benefited through accessibility of welfare programmes.

A study was conducted by **Pavithra R. H (2017)** entitled "An Analysis of Women Welfare Schemes of India". This study was based on the secondary data collected from Books, journals, articles, news papers and internet. The major objectives of this study are to highlight the important women welfare schemes and to suggest suitable measures for effective implementation of such schemes.

Kandpal et al (2012) studied the participation in community level female empowerment programme in India increased participants physical motility, political participation and access to employment.

Sudansu Rath (2008) in his article, "Public Choice, Public Policy and Social Welfare in a Democratic Country: A Theoretical Analysis" felt that Governmental intervention is required in the case of market failure. Public choice, public policy and social welfare concepts are relevant in the context of a democratic welfare state. He also stated that public policy determined by political behaviour misrepresents public choice and deviates from maximum social welfare. Finally, assessment of social welfare and social justice rests on value judgments.

Jeya A. and Kirubakaran Samuel (2010) in their article, "A Study on Impact of Social Welfare Schemes on Rural women in Cuddalore District" dealt with the impact of social welfare schemes on rural women in Tamil Nadu. It also outlined the extent of benefit availed by the rural women based on field survey. The result is that rural women are greatly benefited by the provision of social welfare schemes.

Venkateswarlu (2008) in his article, "Social Security Measures for the Empowerment of the Aged" highlighted the various social security measures provided by the Government in terms of old age pension, old age homes, and mobile geriatric measures, marginal subsidies on train and flight tickets for empowering the old age people.

Most of the previous studies did not conduce as Social Development through Welfare Policies in Karnataka: Special Reference to Marriages Schemes, Hence present study carries on it.

Objectives

To study about Welfare Schemes of social development in Karnataka State

To analyses the Marriage Schemes for social development in Karnataka

Methodology

In this study based on secondary data collected from the census of India, 2011 and social welfare department, Karnataka. There are five marriages schemes have been discussed in this study namely, incentives to Inter Caste Marriages, Intra Caste Marriages, Widow Remarriages, Simple Marriages, and Devadasi Children's Marriage. These welfare policies are initiating to promotion for vulnerable communities.

Date Analyses and Interpretation

Table 1: Distribution of Population in Karnataka, 2011

Sl. No.	*Name of the District*	*Total Population*	*Total SCs Population*	*Total STs Population*
1.	Belgaum	7.8	**5.5**	7.0
2.	Bagalkot	3.1	3.0	2.3
3.	Bijapur	3.6	4.2	0.9
4.	Bidar	2.8	3.8	5.6
5.	Raichur	3.2	3.8	**8.6**
6.	Koppal	2.3	2.5	3.9
7.	Gadag	1.7	1.7	1.5
8.	Dharwad	3.0	1.7	2.1
9.	Uttara Kannada	2.4	1.1	0.8
10.	Haveri	2.6	2.1	3.3
11.	Bellary	4.0	4.9	**10.6**
12.	Chitradurga	2.7	3.7	7.1

(*Contd...*)

13.	Davanagere	3.2	3.7	5.5
14.	Shimoga	2.9	2.9	1.5
15.	Udupi	1.9	0.7	1.2
16.	Chikmagalur	1.9	2.4	1.1
17.	Tumkur	4.4	4.8	4.9
18.	Bangalore	15.7	**11.4**	4.5
19.	Mandya	3.0	2.5	0.5
20.	Hassan	2.9	3.3	0.8
21.	Dakshina Kannada	3.4	1.4	1.9
22.	Kodagu	0.9	0.7	1.4
23.	Mysore	4.9	5.1	7.9
24.	Chamarajanagar	1.7	2.5	2.8
25.	Gulbarga	4.2	6.2	1.5
26.	Yadgir	1.9	2.6	3.5
27.	Kolar	2.5	4.4	1.9
28.	Chikkaballapura	2.1	3.0	3.7
29.	Bangalore Rural	1.6	2.0	1.2
30.	Ramanagara	1.8	1.9	0.5
	Total	100	100	100

Sources: Computed from Primary Census Abstract Data, 2011, Office of the Registrar General & Census Commissioner, Ministry of Home Affairs, Government of India.

In Karnadaka the total Scheduled Castes (SCs) population reported in the district is 11,98,385 persons, constituting about 12.46 percent of total population of the district. The decadal growth rate of Scheduled Castes as per 2011 Census is 40.81 percent. The proportion of Scheduled Castes in the district to total SCs in the State is 11.44 percent. The growth rate of Scheduled Tribes (STs) during the decade 2001-2011 is 121.16 percent and about 1.98 percent of the district's total population are Scheduled Tribes. The share of district's STs to total Scheduled Tribes in the State is 4.48 percent. The decadal change in the growth rate of SCs and STs in urban areas has reported to be very high compared to the growth rate in rural areas as per government data. As per this table reveals that, Bangalore and Belgaum is high proposition for SC and Raichur, Bellary is predominate by the ST community group of people are living.

Inter Caste Marriage

Social Welfare Department, Government of Karnataka Incentive to the Inter Caste Marriage Couple So that anyone from the couple belonging to Schedule Caste along with following criterias: Inter Caste Marriage Incentive is given to SC individual residing in the state of Karnataka to reduce casteism and promote a more accepting society. The incentive is given to a SC resident of Karnataka, who marries a Hindu Non SC individual and where the total income of the couple is less than Rs. 5.0 lakhs.

Table 2: Incentive For Inter Caste Marriage Districtwise Details

Name of the District	*Budget year*				
	2015-2016	*2016-2017*	*2017-2018*	*2018-2019*	*2019-2020*
Belgaum	0	20	**103**	**155**	**131**
Bagalakote	0	7	30	31	42
Bijapur	0	0	14	66	53
Gulbarga	0	1	32	99	197
Bidar	0	0	8	36	38
Raichur	0	1	36	36	46
Koppal	0	4	25	41	35
Gadag	0	8	39	45	38
Dharwad	0	0	**87**	**123**	**115**
Uttara Kannada	0	3	48	74	80
Haveri	0	10	31	75	80
Bellary	0	19	66	107	85
Chitradurga	0	1	81	124	99
Davanagere	0	**19**	**125**	**137**	**146**
Shimoga	0	**29**	**172**	**229**	**221**
Udupi	0	3	31	27	38
Chikmagalore	0	27	**179**	**122**	**153**
Tumkur	0	27	**206**	**221**	**182**
Kolar	0	0	37	148	124
Bangalore Urban	0	**36**	**329**	**747**	**655**
Bangalore Rural	1	15	163	127	128
Mandya	1	15	78	155	116
Hassan	0	8	106	168	173
Dakshina Kannada	0	0	12	34	28
Kodagu	0	6	47	47	48
Mysore	0	**25**	**145**	**283**	**223**
Chamaraja nagar	0	0	26	55	42

(*Contd...*)

Chamaraja nagar	0	0	26	55	42
Ramanagar	0	11	54	111	108
Chikkaballapura	0	0	40	93	100
Yadgir	0	0	17	17	21
Total	2	**295**	**2367**	**3733**	**3545**

Source: Computed from Commissionerate of Social Welfare for the Educational, Social & Economic Upliftment of SCs, Karnataka

Traditionally, marriage in Hindu society was a sacrament but after the passage of Hindu Marriage Act 1955 it can be treated as a contract. However, still marriages primarily take place on the traditional grounds of Jatis (Caste) and Up-Jati (Sub-Caste). That means marriage is inextricably linked to Jati Vyavastha (Caste System) with its roots in the religion. Inter-caste marriages can be one of the significant steps to reduce the caste-prejudices, abolish 'untouchability' as per Indian constitution Article 14 and spread the values of liberty, equality and fraternity in the society. Government of Karnataka took lots of imitative programmes. The above table shows that in 2015-2016 only Bangalore Rural and Mandya was get benifit only 02 member from the inter cast marriage incentive by Government of Karnataka but after 2016 it happing very tramitic changes in particular district like Belgaum, Dharwad, Davanagere, Shimoga, Chikmagalore, Tumkur, Bangalore Urban, Mysore etc., So this table reveals that almost are getting benefit and awareness about the this scheme

Intra Caste Marriage

Intra Caste Marriage Incentive is given to SC individual residing in the state of Karnataka to reduce casteism and promote a more accepting society. The incentive is given to a SC resident of Karnataka, who marries a SC individual and where the total income of the couple is less than Rs. 2.0 lakhs. Social Welfare Department, Government of Karnataka Incentive to the Intra Caste Marriage Couples So that both couple should be SC along with following criteria.

Table 3: Incentive for Intra Caste Marriage District-wise Details

Name of the District	*Budget year*				
	2015-2016	*2016-2017*	*2017-2018*	*2018-2019*	*2019-2020*
Gulbarga	**0**	**0**	**1**	**33**	**67**
Bellary	0	0	1	49	27
Bangalore Urban	**0**	**0**	**0**	**20**	**25**
Belgaum	0	0	8	18	19
Shimoga	0	0	4	15	18
Bangalore Rural	0	0	4	11	18
Chikmagalore	0	0	4	14	15
Chikkaballapura	0	0	3	14	10
Tumkur	0	0	4	11	9
Davanagere	0	0	6	10	10
Bidar	0	0	6	10	5
Chitradurga	0	0	2	10	6
Hassan	0	0	2	6	10
Dharwad	**0**	**0**	**0**	**4**	**13**
Kolar	0	0	2	7	7
Koppal	0	0	0	5	8
Raichur	0	0	2	3	9
Bijapur	0	0	4	4	6
Gadag	0	0	0	6	6
Haveri	0	0	0	2	10
Mysore	0	0	1	7	3
Uttara Kannada	0	0	1	4	4
Mandya	0	0	0	2	4
Ramanagar	0	0	1	4	1
Kodagu	0	0	0	3	2
Dakshina Kannada	0	0	0	4	1
Bagalakote	0	0	1	3	2
Chamaraja nagar	0	0	0	2	1
Udupi	0	0	0	1	1
Yadgir	0	0	0	0	0
Total	**0**	**0**	**57**	**282**	**317**

Source: Computed from Commissionerate of Social Welfare for the Educational, Social & Economic Upliftment of SCs, Karnataka.

This table also emphasizes that, in over all getting number of beneficiary is increased from 2017 to till (2020) by this Incentive for Intra Caste Marriage schemes. Particularly Gulbarga, Bangalore Urban and Dharwad are greater than other states. Its reveals that in this meticulous district have more aware about the schemes. This awareness reflecting about the literary ratio.

Widow Re-Marriage

Social Welfare Department, Government of Karnataka Incentive to The Widow Re-Marriage Widow must be Scheduled Caste along with following criteria's: The Incentive is given to a SC resident of Karnataka, who marries widow there is no caste/religion restrictions/ No Income Limit for Spouse.

Table 4: Incentive For Widow Re-Marriage District-wise Details

Name of the District	*Budget year*				
	2015-2016	*2016-2017*	*2017-2018*	*2018-2019*	*2019-2020*
Gulbarga	**0**	**0**	**0**	**21**	**32**
Mysore	0	0	6	11	12
Belgaum	0	0	1	7	2
Chikkaballapura	0	0	2	2	6
Bidar	0	0	3	6	0
Shimoga	0	0	0	5	4
Bellary	0	0	0	6	2
Bangalore Rural	0	0	1	4	2
Bangalore Urban	0	0	0	2	3
Kolar	0	0	0	3	3
Mandya	0	0	0	5	0
Tumkur	0	0	2	2	1
Davanagere	0	0	2	2	1
Dharwad	**0**	**0**	**0**	**2**	**2**
Hassan	0	0	1	2	1
Chamaraja nagar	0	0	0	3	1
Ramanagar	0	0	0	2	2
Uttara Kannada	0	0	0	1	2
Bagalakote	0	0	1	0	2
Bijapur	0	0	1	1	1
Gadag	0	0	0	2	0
Chikmagalore	0	0	1	0	1
Yadgir	0	0	0	0	2
Udupi	0	0	0	2	0
Raichur	0	0	0	1	1
Dakshina Kannada	0	0	0	0	1
Koppal	0	0	0	1	0
Chitradurga	0	0	0	0	0
Haveri	0	0	0	0	0
Kodagu	0	0	0	0	0
Total	**0**	**0**	**21**	**93**	**84**

Source: Computed from Commissionerate of Social Welfare for the Educational, Social & Economic Upliftment of SCs, Karnataka.

An event that took place around 163 years ago changed the fortune of crores of Indian women. The East India Company passed the Hindu Widows' Remarriage Act, 1856 which legalised the remarriage of Hindu widows on 16th July 1856. This was enacted on 26th July 1856. The law was implemented in all regions under the jurisdictions of East India company in India. This Act, also known as Act XV, 1856 legalised the remarriage of Hindu widows in all the regions which came under the jurisdiction of the East India Company. The Governor-General of India at that time was Lord Canning. This was enacted due to the tireless efforts of social reformer Ishwar Chandra Vidyasagar. The above table shows that in overall analyzed that 2018-2019 to 2019-2020 is number of beneficiary are increasing. According data Gulbarga is top most aware and benefit by the schemes.

Simple Marriage

Social Welfare Department, Government of Karnataka Incentive to the Simple Marriage Couples So that Both the couple should be SC along with following criteria. Scheme is applicable for within a year of marriage. Whose family income is below 2.00 lakhs. Inter Caste Married Couples are not eligible for this scheme. Couples should be residing in Karnataka.

Table 5:Incentive for Simple Marriage District-wise Details.

Name of the District	*Budget year*				
	2015-2016	*2016-2017*	*2017-2018*	*2018-2019*	*2019-2020*
Bellary	0	0	0	277	230
Raichur	0	0	0	182	239
Davanagere	0	0	0	183	123
Gadag	0	0	0	163	55
Koppal	0	0	0	128	71
Yadgir	0	0	0	77	90
Haveri	0	0	0	64	91
Chitradurga	0	0	0	107	41

(*Contd...*)

Bagalakote	0	0	0	86	62
Bijapur	0	0	0	68	80
Chikkaballapura	0	0	0	107	21
Bidar	0	0	0	42	80
Gulbarga	0	0	0	47	70
Belgaum	0	0	0	39	58
Mysore	0	0	0	29	46
Chamaraja nagar	0	0	0	24	42
Bangalore Rural	0	0	0	40	21
Dharwad	0	0	0	22	26
Shimoga	0	0	0	18	21
Udupi	0	0	0	17	16
Mandya	0	0	0	12	19
Chikmagalore	0	0	0	19	2
Tumkur	0	0	0	12	3
Bangalore Urban	0	0	0	9	1
Dakshina Kannada	0	0	0	1	5
Hassan	0	0	0	1	4
Ramanagar	0	0	0	3	2
Uttara Kannada	0	0	0	3	2
Kolar	0	0	0	0	3
Kodagu	0	0	0	0	0
Total	**0**	**0**	**0**	**1780**	**1524**

Source: Computed from Commissionerate of Social Welfare for the Educational, Social & Economic Upliftment of SCs, Karnataka.

The Simple Marriage Incentive schemes also one of the social welfare schemes it is given to SC individual residing in the state of Karnataka to reduce Lots of money, prevent dowry and promote a more accepting society. The incentive is given to an SC resident of Karnataka, who marries another SC individual and where the total income of the couple is less than Rs. 2.0 lakhs. The above table reveals that Bellary, Raichur, Davanagere, Gadag, Koppal, Chitradurga and Chikkaballapura regian get more benefit comparatively to other district, but 2015 to 2018 no one get benefit, after the 2018 by the incentive for simple marriage.

Devadasi Children's Marriage

Social Welfare Department, Government of Karnataka Incentive to the Incentive For The Devadasi's Children's Marriage Couple So that Devadasi belonging to Schedule Caste along with following criterias: Scheme is Applicable for within 18months of marriage for couple belonging to Hindu whose family Income is below 5.0 Lakhs (July 2019) residing in Karnataka.

Table 6: Incentive for Devadasi Children's Marriage District-wise Details

Name of the District	*Budget year*				
	2015-2016	*2016-2017*	*2017-2018*	*2018-2019*	*2019-2020*
Bellary	0	0	0	0	296
Gulbarga	0	0	0	0	145
Koppal	0	0	0	0	119
Raichur	0	0	0	0	110
Bagalakote	0	0	0	0	86
Belgaum	0	0	0	0	70
Bijapur	0	0	0	0	70
Gadag	0	0	0	0	53
Yadgir	0	0	0	0	17
Davanagere	0	0	0	0	12
Dharwad	0	0	0	0	10
Haveri	0	0	0	0	9
Chitradurga	0	0	0	0	6
Bangalore Urban	0	0	0	0	3
Bidar	0	0	0	0	2
Dakshina Kannada	0	0	0	0	1
Hassan	0	0	0	0	0
Bangalore Rural	0	0	0	0	0
Chamaraja nagar	0	0	0	0	0
Chikkaballapura	0	0	0	0	0
Chikmagalore	0	0	0	0	0
Kodagu	0	0	0	0	0
Kolar	0	0	0	0	0
Mandya	0	0	0	0	0
Mysore	0	0	0	0	0
Ramanagar	0	0	0	0	0

(Contd...)

Ramanagar	0	0	0	0	0
Shimoga	0	0	0	0	0
Tumkur	0	0	0	0	0
Udupi	0	0	0	0	0
Uttara Kannada	0	0	0	0	0
Total	**0**	**0**	**0**	**0**	**1009**

Source: Computed from Commissionerate of Social Welfare for the Educational, Social & Economic Upliftment of SCs, Karnataka.

Social Welfare Department, Government of Karnataka Offers incentives for Devadasi Children's Marriage couple of Karnataka state. During 2019-2020 only around 1009 couple get benefited, particularly in Bellary, Gulbarga, Koppal and Raichur region because this picky areas only was more prevalent for this kind of Devadasi system.

Discussions and Conclusion

The developments and changes within the social life have light-emitting diode to alter in the social desires. Therefore, issues and their solutions conjointly amendment the commercial revolution that realised within the eighteenth century had some vital impacts not solely on the economic life however conjointly on scheme. It had been aimed to resolve social issues and guarantee prosperity through social policies, that may be a multidisciplinary field, and consequently, the conception of state emerged. The states, that had liberal considerations and ancient protection functions and reached a robust position with their internationalist approaches, underwent a change amount attributable to the economic and social developments that occurred within the half-moon of the 20th century. The study observed that as per 2001 Census, the total population of Karnataka State is 5.29 crores, of which SC and ST constitute about 86 lakhs and 35 lakhs respectively. The percentage of SC and ST population of the State is 16.20% and 6.6% respectively. The literacy rate among SC is 52.90% and ST is 48.31% as against the general literacy of 67.04%. To implement various schemes and programmes, both Central and State Government provide funds. Though some of the schemes are funded either wholly or partly by the Central Government through the Special Central Assistance, Centrally sponsored Schemes under Special Component Plan and Tribal Sub Plan, majority of the schemes are funded and implemented by State Government alone. The schemes are implemented broadly at three different levels, one at State level (Social Welfare Commissionerate), other at District level (Zilla Panchayat) and few at the Taluk Panchayat level. These schemes cover the main priority sectors; Education, Employment, Housing, Irrigation, and so on.

Social welfare policy provides a much-needed lifeline for families or people UN agency are either in economic condition or at risk of falling below the poverty level. It's vital not simply within the us however all round the world. If we have a tendency to settle for that basic human rights embrace access to water, food, and shelter, then welfare policy goes a protracted thanks to providing these basic wants for people that would otherwise not have access to them.

There is conjointly a secondary profit to welfare policy that could be a reduction in crime. If a family living off welfare edges suddenly had these benefits abstracted from them, then that family might understand there to be no different choice than to resort to petty crime so as to remain alive. Social welfare policy is extremely vital as a result of welfare ought to be viewed as means that to associate degree finish, not the tip itself. Government of Karnataka has been spending lot of money to promotion of equalitarian society.

In 2019-2020 more couples applied for incentives to Inter Caste Marriages, Intra Caste Marriages, Widow Remarriages, Simple Marriages, and Devadasi Children's Marriages. It means that government has initiated good effort to the development of SCs/STs and other vulnerable communities.

References

1. Commissionerate of Social Welfare for the Educational, Social & Economic Upliftment of SCs, Karnataka.
2. http://home.karnataka.gov.in/en/Pages/Home.aspx
3. Kandpal, E et. al (2012): "Empowering Women through Education and Influence: An Evaluation of the Indian Mahila Samakhya Program". IZA Discussion Paper No. 6347.
4. Primary Census Abstract Data, 2011, Office of the Registrar General & Census Commissioner, Ministry of Home Affairs, Government of India.
5. Rashmi Rani Agnihotri H. R., et. al. (2017): "A Study on Women Empowerment Programmes in Karnataka State: A Theoretical Overview", International Journal of Scientific and Research Publications, Vol. 7, Issue 1, January, pp. 293-298.
6. Sudansu Rath (2008): "Public choice, Public Policy and Social Welfare in a Democratic Country: A Theoretical Analysis", International Journal of Economics, Serials publications, New Delhi, Vol.2, No.2, December, pp. 93-101.
7. Venkateswarlu, V (2008): "Social Security Measures for the Empowerment of the Aged", HRD Times, Chennai, December, pp. 25-26.

Index

T